THE HISTORY OF NFL

First published in 2019
by Murray Books (Australia)
www.murraybooks.com

Copyright © 2019 Murray Books (Australia)
Copyright © 2019 Peter Murray
Licensed to G2 Entertainment UK

ISBN 978-78281-487-0

All rights reserved. This publication or any part thereof may not be reproduced, stored in a retrieval system or transmitted, in any form or by any means, electronic, mechanical, photocopying, recording or otherwise, without the prior written permission of the copyright holder.

Compiled by Peter Murray and Kim Irvine

Images: Shutterstock : AP Images

The author and publisher have made every effort to ensure the information contained in this book was correct at the time of going to press and accept no responsibility for any loss, injury or inconvenience sustained by any person or organisation using this book. Some editorial and images may have been used from the Public Domain.

CONTENTS

4	The History of NFL		84	Denver Broncos
6	The Beginnings of Professional Football		86	Kansas City Chiefs
10	A new league is born		88	Los Angeles Chargers
14	The NFL and American Football League (AFL) Merger		90	Oakland Raiders
20	Modern Day NFL		92	Dallas Cowboys
22	NFL International Expansion		94	New York Giants
24	The popularity of the NFL		96	Philadelphia Eagles
28	**NRL HALL OF FAME**		98	Washington Redskins
28	Jim Brown		100	Chicago Bears
30	Jerry Rice		102	Detroit Lions
34	Lawrence Taylor		104	Green Bay Packers
36	Walter Payton		106	Minnesota Vikings
40	Tom Brady		108	Atlanta Falcons
42	Joe Montana		110	Carolina Panthers
46	Reggie White		112	New Orleans Saints
50	Peyton Manning		114	Tampa Bay Buccaneers
52	Don Hutson		116	Arizona Cardinals
56	Dick Butkus		118	Los Angeles Rams
58	Brett Favre		120	San Francisco 49ers
60	**TEAMS OF THE NFL**		122	Seattle Seahawks
60	Buffalo Bills		124	**STADIUMS OF THE NFL**
62	Miami Dolphins		156	**NFL CURRENT TOP 10**
64	New England Patriots		156	Tom Brady
66	New York Jets		157	Antonio Brown
68	Baltimore Ravens		158	Carson Wentz
70	Cincinnati Bengals		159	Julio Jones
72	Cleveland Browns		160	le'Von Bell
74	Pittsburg Steelers		161	Todd Gurley
76	Houston Texans		162	Aaron Donald
78	Indianapolis Colts		163	Drew Brees
80	Jacksonville Jaguars		164	Von Miller
82	Tennessee Titans		164	Aaron Rodgers

THE HISTORY OF NFL

The NFL was founded as the American Professional Football Association or APFA in 1920. The Association consisted of ten regional league teams from four participating states. It was not until 1922 that the name was changed to the National Football League after which it went on to be the first league to gain nationwide team participation success. While the Green Bay Packers can boast the title of the oldest franchised team in the NFL that has had the same home field since inception. They are not the oldest remaining team still playing in the league to date having only joined in 1921. The Arizona Cardinals once the Chicago Cardinals along with the Chicago Bears once Decatur Staley's share the title as the only remaining founding teams still active in the league.

As the league continued to grow it became a more formal organization as its league memberships started to stabilize from the 1920s through the 1930s. In 1933 the first official NFL Championship game was played. This game would go down as the best game of the year, but it would also be noted for its lack of black players after the NFL unofficially stopped signing them.

The end of World War Two saw some major changes to the league's internal governing body structure. The league president was exalted to a more prominent seat of power as the league Commissioner. The position aligned with the offices of various other major sporting league structures such as Major League Baseball. In 1946 the NFL started to once again sign black players. By 1950 the leagues toughest competitor the All-America Football Conference had folded and most of their teams were integrated into the NFL.

The 1958 NFL's season championship game became one of the most remembered football games to have been played in history. It was dubbed as "The Greatest Game Ever Played" boosting the NFL to become one of America's most popular sports leagues.

In 1960 a new rival for the NFL's sports league success was formed. The American Football League which proved to be a major success throughout the country. The AFL ran in direct competition to the NFL for six years before a merger was agreed upon by the two leagues in 1966. This culminated in the creation of one of America's biggest annual sporting events the Super Bowl. Super Bowl I was played on the 15th January 1967 on the heels of the 1966 regular football seasons finally for both the AFL and NFL. Initially, the Super Bowl was intended as a playoff between the NFL and AFL champion teams until the finalization of the merger in 1970. Today the Super Bowl is all but considered as an unofficial national holiday in America by its staunch supporters. Super Bowl Sunday has gone on to frequently top the most watched sporting event each year in America. **The Green Bay Packers (NFL) took home the first-ever Super Bowl title beating the Kansas City Chiefs (AFL) 35-10 (right).**

THE HISTORY OF NFL

Today the league has expanded to a size of thirty-two teams and remains one of the most profitable football leagues due to various television contracts. Its well-devised labor agreements in the 1990s have assured no regularly scheduled game losses due to work stoppages.

The Beginnings of Professional Football

Known as gridiron football because of the fields vertical yard lines that are similar to that of the English sports of football and rugby. The game of American football as it is known today got it starts as a game played by universities in the United States.

Professional football was first started when the Allegheny Athletic Association (of Western Pennsylvania Senior Independent Football conference) offered two football players, namely Ben Donnelly and William Heffelfinger, each a hefty paycheck to play for the Association. The late nineteenth century through to the early part of the twentieth century had most football games being played regionally with very few games played against another state. It was not for a lack of trying to get a national league started such as the first NFL which has no affiliation with the current NFL. The First attempt at the NFL was started in 1902 and was backed by an association that would become Major League Baseball. The league managed to have two World Series of Pro Football tournaments before they were disbanded. There seemed to be no fan base interest in any of the attempts made to create new football circuits or combine the already established ones. The attempts at national leagues were up against heavily organized regional football circuits with their strong loyal supporting fan base. These leagues included the extremely well-organized New York Pro Championship League and the Ohio League that was home to the legendary Native American player and athlete Jim Thorpe.

In 1917 two of New York States teams, the Buffalo All-Stars and the Rochester Jefferson's traveled to Ohio for a barnstorming tour. It was here that Leo Lyons, who at the time owned the Rochester Jefferson's, got the idea of forming a league that would rival if not outdo the popularity of baseball. Baseball dominated the professional sporting circuits in the early 1900s in America. After the Jefferson's lost to the Canton Bulldogs of which **Jim Thorpe (right)** both played and coached Lyons suggested the formation of a national league to him.

Lyon's idea for the formation of a new national football league came up against quite a few obstacles in the early stages of life. Such as another proposed football league that was once again to be backed by a

THE HISTORY OF NFL

baseball league. Then there was a flu epidemic outbreak in 1918 and his vision was further upended by America's participation in World War I. Most of the Ohio league players were hampered by war drafts of their players or strict travel restrictions that were put in place due to the flu. As a result, Ohio was put in the difficult situation of having to suspend all operations as they lost valuable players.

Despite all the restrictions and drafting's a few teams in New York still remained playing to a much-reduced schedule but still managed to survive the suspension. Some of these remaining teams were the Detroit Heralds from Michigan and Dayton Ohio's Dayton Triangles. These teams accommodated the absorption of as many of the star football players from suspended teams that remained on US soil as possible.

The Great Lakes Navy Bluejacket football team (right) consisting of some players that would become football hall of famers, played against college football teams for the 1919 Rose Bowl and won. Paddy Driscoll, Jimmy Conzelman and George Halas not only served together but lead the Bluejackets to win the 1919 Rose Bowl. This saw a clear shift in the spreading of talent across larger geographical areas. Throughout 1919 professional football started to become further organized and more teams took to barnstorming tours. This also saw the rise of an informal Eastern Seaboard and Midwestern region circuits. The Midwestern regions which included Indiana, Minnesota, Wisconsin, Illinois, and upstate New York would play on Sunday. The second circuit was the Eastern Seaboard which encompassed teams from New Jersey, Philadelphia and New York City played on a Saturday in order to adhere to the blue laws. The NFL as it is known today was founded by the teams from the Midwestern circuit.

It was in the face of yet some more bidding wars threatening to erupt that teams in Ohio opted to go along with the formation of a national league. Having had bidding wars already significantly cause teams in both Ohio and Pennsylvania a lot of damage. These bidding wares were also costly and there was no telling if the sport would survive another round. Drastic steps had to be taken in order to stop the poaching of team's best players leaving them vulnerable. A league would ensure that top players were evenly distributed throughout the teams. Leveling out the playing fields and reducing costs per team as they would not be put in a position where they had to stretch their coffers to keep their star players.

THE HISTORY OF NFL

A new league is born

It was in Canton, Ohio at a Hupmobile dealership that the American Professional Football Conference was formed on the 20th August 1920. The initial league members consisted of most of the Ohio League teams with a few of Ohio's teams choosing not to join. The league expanded to include Rochester and Buffalo (from the New York League), Hammond (Chicago Squad team) and Detroit. The recruiting of these teams coincided with the renaming of the league to the American Professional Football Association on the 17th September 1920. At this time the squad consisted of eleven teams with Jim Thorpe playing for the Bulldogs. He was elected the first president of the APFA. **That same year the Akron Pros (right) were the first team to win the new championship and only four of the eleven original league teams actually finished the schedule for the year.**

The Leagues membership continued to grow and by 1921 it had twenty-two participating teams which included more league teams from New York. The league had little national acclaim throughout the 1920s and still could not boast to being a major national sport. The league's membership, although having increased substantially, was still not very stable. The New Hayden Building in Columbus, Ohio became the league's headquarters and on June the 24th 1922, it once again undertook a name change to become the National Football League (NFL).

The NFL has seen many franchises over the years with two of the original founding member teams still in play today. The Chicago Bears who were originally the Decatur Stanleys and the Arizona Cardinals who were the Chicago Cardinals have been with the league since its inception in 1920. The Green Bay Packers who were founded as the Green Bay Acme Packers in 1919 only started playing with the league in 1921. They are the only team in the league to have never changed location. In 1925 the New York Football Giants (known as the New York Giants) became members of the NFL with the Portsmouth Spartans joining not long after in 1930. The Spartans since became the Lions after being relocated to Detroit in 1934. Some of the original NFL League teams from the Cleveland, Chicago, Detroit, and Buffalo regions that have since folded still hold representation from new franchises in the areas. Such as the Indianapolis Colts that started as the Baltimore Colts and have some of the roots in founding teams such as the Dayton Triangles.

Most of the early championships winners were determined by the teams that had the best win-loss rate. This was not very fair when some teams got to play more games than other teams in the league did. The lack of a clearly organized structure within the then APFA became clear as some teams were scheduled to play games against non-league teams, collegiate or amateur teams. This resulted in the need of a tiebreaker

THE HISTORY OF NFL

in 1921, which was only the second regular APFA season. The structure had not changed much within the newly organized NFL which became clear in 1925 with a title dispute and a need for an impromptu playoff in 1932 that had to be scheduled in an indoor arena. Teams were being constantly added to and removed from the leagues yearly roster. Franchises were haphazardly bought and sold at the whim of a team owner in order to get the team's star player folding the team once they got the rights to the player. The New York Giants took over the Wolverines in 1928 in order to gain the rights to Benny Friedman before folding the Wolverines. Owners of franchises in one city were known to trade for one in another city such as what happened to the Detroit Wolverines, Canton Bulldogs, and the Cleveland Bulldogs.

Three new teams were admitted to the NFL in 1933 they were the Eagles, Pirates and the Cincinnati Reds. The NFL now consisted of ten league teams and through pressure from some of the league's team owners it was decided to split the league into two divisions. The Western Division that would have the Chicago Bears, Chicago Cardinals, Cincinnati Reds, Green Bay Packers, and the Portsmouth Spartans. The Eastern Division which consisted of the **New York Giants (right)**, The Pittsburgh Pirates, Boston Redskins, Brooklyn Dodgers and Philadelphia Eagles. George Halas and George Preston Marshall, the original driving forces between the split divisions, further convinced the league into forming an NFL Championship Game which would be a playoff between the two divisions season winners.

Most of the smaller town league teams with the exception of the Green Bay Packers had either been replaced by larger city teams or had their teams uprooted to a bigger city by 1934. With pressure on teams to gain more spectator support in order to keep the teams from folding or being swallowed by larger ones, even the Green Bay Packers started to play more home games in the larger Milwaukee Stadium. The corporate headquarters of the NFL itself was moved from Columbus, Ohio to Chicago in 1941.

Most of the early league teams took their names from other well-known major sporting league teams. In particular that of the Major Baseball League teams such as the Cincinnati Reds, Brooklyn Dodgers, New York Yankees, Buffalo Bison's, Pittsburgh Pirates, Detroit Tigers, and Cleveland Indians.

The 1930s saw a few changes in the NFL with it holding its first ever annual college football player draft in 1936. The Dodgers won over the Eagles of 23-14 at Ebbets field on the 22 October 1939 became the first ever televised NFL game. The Boston Braves joined the NFL in 1932 bringing with them its owner George Preston Marshall. Marshall went on to be the instigated of many changes in the NFL including that of player segregation in 1933. In order to appease their Southern Supporters many an NFL team owner

13

THE HISTORY OF NFL

followed Marshalls whites-only policy with a result there were no black professional football players until the 1950s. Even after the policy was overturned Marshall refused to let any blacks into his team the Washington Redskins. His policy for his team was upheld until the team was forced to become integrated in 1962 during the Kennedy administration.

George Preston Marshall for all his bigotry still managed to make some great contributions to the NFL such as championship games, better-fixed scheduling and separate conferences. It is for this reason that he is a charter member of the Pro Football Hall of Fame.

Professional football started to rival the more popular college football by the end of World War II. Fans were beginning to move towards supporting the professional games especially as rule changes in the games started to give way to a faster game with T-Formation innovations and games that gave higher scoring rates. By 1945 the league had expanded from just the Midwest with the transfer of the Cleveland Rams to Los Angeles the league got a foot in on the West Coast. In 1949 the All-American Football Conference folded, and the NFL took three of its teams the San Francisco 49ers, Baltimore Colts and the Cleveland Browns on board in 1950. It was during this year that the NFL once again changed its name to the National-American Football League. But the name only stuck for three months before it was changed back the National Football League.

The championship game that was dubbed the "Greatest Game Ever Played" in the NFL history was in 1958. It was the first ever nationally televised NFL game played between the New York Giants and the Baltimore Colts (right). The game was one that kept the spectators on their seats culminating in a spectacular ending. This was the game that put the NFL on the road to becoming one of the most popular sporting leagues in America and earning professional football its rightful place as a major sport.

The NFL and American Football League (AFL) Merger

The NFL struggled to regain its foothold in 1946 after World War II and the stress especially with the pressure of the AFL (was the American Association that renamed itself to the American Football League after WWII) the commissioner of the NFL, Elmer Layden stepped down. Bert Bell was elected as the commissioner thereafter accepting the position with the condition that the headquarters for the NFL was moved to Philadelphia. Bert Bell had a valuable impact on the NFL from the time he took over as commissioner until his untimely death at Franklin Field where he had a heart attack during the Steelers-

THE HISTORY OF NFL

Eagles game in 1959. Bell had transformed the NFL into a huge commercial success and had gained the league increased popularity. It was not too long after the death of Burt Bell that the NFL's head offices were once again moved. This time they were moved to Manhattan where they still remain today.

Throughout most of the 1950s, the NFL reigned as the most popular league for professional football. Even with the inception of new leagues threatening their popularity at least once a year the league kept its professional football status unchallenged. That was until a group of would-be football owners got fed up with being turned down on their efforts to buy into the NFL. The group that included some minority franchise owners in the NFL such as Ralph Wilson and Harry Wiseman along with Bud Adams and Lamar Hunt started a new AFL league in 1960. This league was in no means associated with any of the previous leagues known as the American Football League. Even though the group soon became known as the "Foolish Club" they were the fourth club that stood to challenge the NFL's standing in the pro football scene. They also proved to be the most formidable challengers in the NFL's history.

The AFL soon started to compete with the NFL for players and this included the annual college drafts. The war for players between the two leagues soon started to drive up players' salaries and in 1965 the AFL scored one over the NFL when they signed **quarterback Joe Namath (right)** who passed over the St. Louis Cardinals (NFL) for the New York Jets (AFL). He signed with the AFL for record earnings of the era of $427,000. Competition between the leagues escalated until in 1966 the New York Giants (NFL) signed one of the Buffalo Bills (AFL) placekickers, Pete Gogolak. The Giants had broken what was a silent agreement between the leagues and pouched one of the AFL's star players. The AFL retaliated as then Commissioner Al Davis went on a mission to sign up as many of the NFL top players as he could. He was especially interested in the star quarterbacks of the NFL's best teams. As Davis embarked on his campaign against the NFL some of the NFL franchise owners were already deliberating on a way to end this rivalry against the leagues that was sorely threatening their teams.

Tex Schramm, who at the time was the General Manager of the Cowboys headed up the NFL committee that met with the AFL in order to negotiate a merger between the two leagues. The mergers agreement was brokered by Schramm and Hunt (the founder of the AFL) which was announced on the 8th June 1966. It was agreed that with the merger there would be some common ground such as a common annual draft and a World Championship game that would end the season and would be played between the two leagues. The World Championship Game became known as the Super Bowl I and proved to be an outstanding

THE HISTORY OF NFL

success. **To date, the Superbowl remains one of the most watched sporting events in America with fans proclaiming Super Bowl Sunday as an unofficial holiday (right).**

New Orleans was given an NFL franchise from the efforts of the AFL and Louisiana federal Congressmen that managed to push for the passing of Public Law 89-900 ultimately allowing for the merger and exempting Anti-Trust restrictions. As a monopoly would be created with the merger it would need an act of Congress to legitimize it. The merger was cleared with the two leagues merging under the NFL's name in 1970. The NFL was divided into two different conferences each conference would have an equal number of teams. Since the NFL had six more teams than the AFL three of its team were moved to the AFC (AFL Division of the NFL). The teams that were moved over were the Baltimore Colts, the Pittsburgh Steelers and the Cleveland Browns. There were two other teams that were added to the NFL as part of the merger deal, but they did not play in the league until 1976 due to their home stadiums not being able to accommodate the larger more well-known teams. Once the Tampa Bay Buccaneers and the Seattle Seahawks had successfully commissioned bigger more suitable stadiums, they each gained a franchise into the NFL along with a settlement figure of $18 million paid over 20 years to the AFL teams.

The AFL may have lost its identity to the NFL, but a lot of the league's policies were taken on by the NFL. Such as the wide-open offensive rules, southern franchises, a game clock on the field, the player's jerseys sporting their names, sharing the money made from television and gate sales and drafting from the smaller more predominantly black colleges.

The NFL may not have been able to do much about stopping players being drafted into World War I and World War II. But concerted efforts by both the NFL and AFL helped save many a football player from being sent to Vietnam during the war. This was done by the adoption of champagne units which kept their players from being deployed overseas instead they got to serve in lower risk duties or the National Guard inside the borders of the United States. Only one of the AFL's players died in combat, Bob Kalsu of the Buffalo Bills who left the team to serve his country in the war. An NFL veteran, Don Steinbrunner, who had left pro football (played for the Cleveland Browns) for over ten years before the war in Vietnam also died over there in combat.

THE HISTORY OF NFL

Modern Day NFL

The 1970s saw the NFL become America's number one spectator sport and was soon embedded into the America Culture. With the success of the Superbowl and the Monday Night Football series that became one of America's top-rated TV-shows 1970 drastically turned things around for pro football. With the new clever mix of Television sports and entertainment as well as various football rule changes to ensure the game gave the fans lots of fast-paced action and passings American's were soon glued to the sport.

The NFL has had a few challenges for dominance as the top sports league in America after the AFL **the next threat to challenge them was the World Football League which was started in 1974 (right)**. Although due to financial difficulties it did not last very long it still managed to lure away some of the NFL's top players. It also brought about the need for a few rules to be changed within the NFL. The WFL played for one whole season and could not financially sustain itself folding mid-way through its second season. Two of its team unsuccessfully tried to join the NFL after the WFL folded these teams were the Memphis Southmen and the Birmingham Vulcans.

The next major challenge to the NFL's Dominance came in the form of the United States Football League founded in 1974. One of its founding members being Donald Trump. Although the well-funded USFL flaunted some of the big-name players and lucrative national TV deal the league made a grave error in trying to go up against the NFL in a head-to-head in the fall instead of keeping its spring niche. The USFL was already over-spent on the acquiring of its players and the USFL folded after giving the NFL a good run for its money for three consecutive seasons. In order to try and save the league, the USFL went on to sue the NFL for anti-trust damages. They failed to acquire the hundreds of million dollars they were suing for. With no funds, the league folded but it created a feud that has spanned three decades between Donald Trump and the NFL. In 2014 Donald Trumps failed attempt to purchase the Buffalo Bills franchise has only fueled his angst against the NFL even more. This hostility has bled into the Trump administration and his ire towards the 2016 national anthem protests.

Vince McMahon together with a disgruntled NBC that lost the NFL broadcast rights started another football league meant to challenge the NFL in 2001, XFL could not sustain itself financially and folded after only one season without any impact on the NFL. One thing the XFL did do was to relaunch the careers of former NFL players. It also brought about some innovative sports presentations breathing creativity into sports entertainment of which McMahon fully intend to use to his advantage when he attempts to relaunch XFL in 2020.

THE HISTORY OF NFL

In 2009 the United Football League has formed once again it was yet another league that was going to directly challenge the NFL's status. The league never went forward with its plans to have teams in Los Angeles and New York offering salaries that were competitive with those of the NFL. Instead, it opted to cut salaries and took on a more complementary approach taking on teams in Omaha, Las Vegas and Sacramento. After sustaining huge financial losses the UFL folded. The NFL has been challenged by many leagues over the years, but none have yet to make a dent in the NFL's popularity and some have not even made it to the first game.

The league made changes to its logo for the first time since 1980 in August 2007 which was used in the 2008 season. The changes showed that there were now only eight stars, one for each of the league's division as opposed to the former twenty-five. The NFL lettering was changed from Italic to a straight serif font and that the football was shaped/positioned as the Vince Lombardi Trophy. The digitally designed logo was created for TV, media, clothing, and memorabilia although the shield logo dating back as far as the 1940s.

NFL International Expansion

In 1986 the NFL held some exhibition games outside of the United States in its venture into new international markets. This started with a series known as the American Bowl which ran which started in 1986. The American Bowl was held at various countries around the world before the league shut the games down in 2005. The NFL started the World League of American Football in 1991 which soon became known as NFL Europe and then NFL Europa. This league was a developmental one that had teams in countries such as Spain, Germany, the Netherlands, and Britain (opposite). The NFL Europa was ended by the NFL in 2007.

In 2005 the NFL took to playing one regular game of the season in Mexico City. This started was marketed as the Fútbol Americano game. This became the first regular season NFL game to be played outside the USA in the NFL's history. The Miami Dolphins played the New York Giants for a regular season game in the **Wembley Stadium (right)** in London in 2008. This game sold over forty thousand tickets just minutes after the tickets went on sale. Gameday at Wembley Stadium saw an attendance of over 80000 fans. After that, the Tampa Bay Buccaneers played the New England Patriots in 2009 at Wembley and in 2010 the San Francisco 49ers played the Denver Broncos at the Wembley Stadium. The Buffalo Bills play an annual game in Toronto at the Rogers Center and it is called the "Bills Toronto Series" which started from the

THE HISTORY OF NFL

2008/09 seasons. The Atlanta Falcons played the Detroit Lions as an away game of the 2014 series at Wembley Stadium. Estadio Azteca in Mexico was host to the 2016 season game between the Texans and the Raiders with the Raiders returning to this stadium in 2017 to play against the Patriots.

Due to its close proximity to the States and a hundred years of football influence in America the NFL wisely identified Mexico as a key market outside of America. This, in turn, led to the NFL opening expanding its presence into Mexico by opening up an office there called NFL Mexico. The office is solely responsible for its own public relations, various community services, sponsorships and licensing.

The popularity of the NFL

Baseball may be "America's national pastime" but football tops it as the nations most loved spectator sport. From 1965 when the NFL was challenged by the competition of the AFL pro football climbed to the top of America's favorite league's sports to watch.

According to various polls such as the Harris Poll, ESPN Sports Poll and various studies that were conducted by the Sports Marketing group pro football has remained America's top spectator sport. The Harris Poll which was taken in 2008 showed that 30 percent of people loved football as compared to 15% for baseball, 10% for automobile racing and 2% for hockey. According to the poll, football lovers equal the combined total of all the other popular sports.

On Television, football has higher viewer ratings than any other sport even though it has fewer season games than a lot of other sports. Other polls such as the ESPN Sports Poll and the studies taken by Sports Marketing Group that were run from 1988 through 2004 show the NFL coming in at a much higher most popular spectator sport than the Harris Poll. These other polls tend to compare the sport to many more sports. The AP who released the Sports Marketing Groups findings in the most detailed ever take of the American sports lovers favored sports. There were 114 different sports that the survey listed that people may want to attend and still the NFL came in above all the other sports with 39% of Americans saying they would choose to either go to a stadium game, read about it or watch it on the TV.

When it comes to game attendance the NFL gets the "highest per-game attendance" than any other professional sports league throughout the world. As Baseball has a 132-game schedule compared to the much shorter schedule of the NFL it tends to have a much higher overall attendance rate. The NFL has

THE HISTORY OF NFL

only around 20% of the attendance than Major League Baseballs does in a season.

The NFL got ranked in the top twenty-five out of one-hundred and twenty-two for "team loyalty" in the Turnkey Team Brand Index for 2007. The NFL teams that ranked tops in the index came in as follows:

At the top was the Pittsburgh Steelers with their loyal fans, next was the New England Patriots followed by the Indianapolis Colts, New Orleans Saints at number seven and the Green Bay Packers with their loyal fans at number ten. Out of one-hundred and twenty-two teams, the Arizona Cardinals came in right at the bottom. This may have changed since the Arizona Cardinals it to the Super Bowl XLVIII where they played a close game against the Pittsburgh Steelers.

NFL HALL OF FAME

Jim Brown

Career

James Brown was a running back for the Cleveland Browns from 1957 to 1965. He never missed a game in his nine NFL seasons stunning the sports world with his incredible athletic skills. He was the rushing yard lead for eight of his nine career seasons and received the AP NFL Most Valuable Player award three times. In 1964 he won an NFL Championship with the Cleveland Browns and by retirement in 1965 he had broken many of the leagues and team records.

Jim was inducted into the Hall of Fame in 1971 and in 2002 The Sporting News named him as footballs greatest professional player ever.

Personal Information
Born James Nathanial Brown on February 17, 1936, on St. Simons Island, Georgia. He moved to Manhasset, Nassau County, New York at the age of 8. He attended Manhasset High School and it was here that he started his legendary athletic career.

Jim not only excelled in football during his high school career but was also a much-revered basketball, baseball, and lacrosse.

He chose football as his professional sporting career and was drafted to the NFL in 1957, Round number 1 and overall pick number 6. He played for the Cleveland Browns from 1957 through to 1965 where at the age of 30 he announced his retirement from football shocking the nation and his fans.

He went on to be an actor and has appeared in some top movies such Any Given Sunday during his acting career.

Early Years
Brown attended Syracuse University where he was a top athlete in track, lacrosse, basketball, and football. He played for the Syracuse Orangemen Football team where he broke many records and in his senior year (1956) he was the first-team All-American. He was inducted into the College Football Hall of Fame in 1995.

Jim Brown is not only a football hall of famer either he was also inducted into the Lacrosse Hall of Fame. In his junior college year he was named the basketball second-team All-American and in 1955 at the Nation Championship Decathlon, he placed fifth.

His image is forever portrayed at the Carrier Dome where an 800 square-foot tapestry emblazoned with "Greatest Player Ever" is hung. The tapestry shows Jim Brown in both his lacrosse and football uniforms.

NFL HALL OF FAME

Jerry Rice

Career

Jerry Rice is a wide receiver that played for the NFL from 1985 to 2005 in his career he has scored 1,256 points which are more than any other non-kicker player in the league. He played in the NFL league for twenty seasons most of which were spent with the San Francisco 49ers and holds over one-hundred NFL records (as at 2017).

He was inducted into the Pro-football Hall of Fame in 2010. He was selected thirteen times for the Pro Bowl, won three Super Bowls (whilst with the 49ers), was instrumental in the Oakland Raiders winning an AFC Championship and has twelve All-Pro's.

He was listed second (to Jim Brown) as "Footballs 100 Greatest Players" by The Sporting News.

Rice's professional football career was started off with the San Francisco 49ers who chose him regardless of his initial struggle with dropping of passes the 49ers saw promise in him in his rookie season. He did not disappoint them and was named NFC Offensive Rookie of the Year (United Press International). He recorded 49 catches for 927 yards in his rookie season which is an average of 18.9 yards per catch.

The following season saw him excel even more as he went on to lead the league in receiving yards and touchdowns. He was the NFL's MVP in 1987 (named by the Newspaper Enterprise Association and the Pro Football Writers Association). He was also awarded the NFL Player of the Year by the Maxwell Football Club who presented him with the Bert Bell Award.

He joined the Oakland Raiders in 2001 for four seasons, before going onto the Seattle Seahawks for in 2004 and then Denver Broncos in 2005 where he signed for a one-year deal but decided to retire instead.

In 2006 on August the 24th Rice signed a one-day contract with the 49ers so he could officially retire a member of the initial team he had been drafted into for the NFL. The contract was for $1,985,806.49. Although he did not get any money from it the amount symbolized the date, he joined the team, the number of his team jersey, his retirement year and the team name.

Personal Information

Born Jerry Lee Rice Sr he was born in Starkville, Mississippi on the 13th October 1962. He attended Moor High School in Oktoc, Mississippi where initially his mother would not allow him to play football. In his sophomore year, Jerry was caught playing truant by his principal but took off before he could officially be caught. Noting his speed the principal informed the football coach of the school who recruited Jerry to the school's football team.

NFL HALL OF FAME

Football was not the only sport that Jerry was good as he also did field and track as well as basketball.

Two years after he was drafted to the NFL, he married Jacqueline Mitchell with whom he had three children. His youngest son, Jerry Jnr. Plays wide receiver for Rebels. Jerry and Jaqueline divorced in July of 2007 and it was finalized in December of 2009. He became engaged to longtime girlfriend Latisha Pelayo in 2018.

Early Years
After starting football in high school Rice was noticed by a few college football scouts but decided to go to Mississippi Valley State University. During his college years, he managed 4692 receiving yards as well as eighteen Division I-AA records.

He was the overall pick number sixteen in the first round of the 1985 NFL Draft by the San Francisco 49ers. Over his twenty-season career for which he mostly played with the 49ers, he racked up numerous NFL records and retired as a 49er having played 303 career games.

NFL HALL OF FAME

Lawrence Taylor

Career

Lawrence Taylor was a linebacker for the New York Giants from his NFL draft in 1981 through to his retirement in 1993. He became part of what was known as "The Big Blue Wrecking Crew" that the Giants defense became known as they led the team to win Super Bowl XXI and Super Bowl XXV.

Taylor along with his fellow linebacker teammates became known as the best NFL linebacking corps in the league throughout the 1980s. In his rookie season, he took home many defensive awards and brought about changes in NFL such as offensive line play, offensive formations and pass rushing schemes. In every season he played he delivered double-digit sacks producing 20.5 in 1986 which was an all-time career high for him.

Taylor won the NFL MVP award in 1986 making him one of only two defensive players to ever have won this award and no defensive player has won it since. He also took home the AP NFL Defensive Player of the Year award a record three times during his career. In 1983 he became the first ever NFL player to be named as the First-Team All-Pro for two positions which were inside and outside linebacker. He was named First-Team All-Pro each season in his first nine NFL career seasons.

He retired having played for the New York Giants all through is NFL Career in 1993 and was inducted into the Hall of Fame in 1999.

Personal Information

Born February 4, 1959, in Williamsburg, Virginia Lawrence Julius Taylor, nicknamed LT attended Lafayette High School. He is the oldest son in his family with two younger brothers and was referred to as Lonnie by his family. As a child, his mother referred to him as challenging as he was always up to mischievous.

His sport was baseball in which he played the position of catcher right up until he was 15 years old when he started to play football. He only started to play organized football at the age of 16 whilst in the eleventh grade and as such was not really on the radar of any college football scouts.

Early Years

He graduated from high school in 1977 and enrolled in the University of North Carolina, Chapel Hill. It was here that he became the football team captain wearing the number 98 jersey. The first football position he played was as a defensive lineman, he only started to play as a linebacker in 1979 where he managed to accumulate 16 sacks in 1980 which was his final varsity year. He managed to set quite a few records throughout his varsity football career where he was recognized as first-team All-American. In 1980 he was named the Atlantic Coast Conference Player of the year. His coaches all labeled him as one of the most reckless players they had seen with his style of play. He was known to be able to jump at least six foot in the air in order to block a punt before landing on his neck.

He was recruited into the NFL Draft in 1981 in the first round as the second overall pick. He became the linebacker for the New York Giants wearing jersey number 56 and spent his entire pro-football career with the team.

NFL HALL OF FAME

Walter Payton

Career

Walter Payton was known as "Sweetness", a running back for the Chicago Bears he held numerous records for touchdowns, rushing yards, yards from scrimmage amongst a mentioned few. Upon his retirement in 1987, he held the record for most receptions by a non-receiver. Mike Dita, an NFL coach also once a player for the league went of the describe Payton as not only one of the greatest players ever but also a great human being.

When Gale Sayers retired in 1972 the Bears hit a losing streak the Chicago Bears recruited Payton in the first round, overall pick number 4 of the 1975 NFL draft. He may not have had the best starting season, but he did end it by leading the league in yards per kickoff return that year.

In the 1976 NFL season, Payton's game was much improved as he worked hard through the season ending it with 13 scored touchdowns and rushed for 1390 yards. He won was named the Pro Bowl MVP after being selected for the 1977 Pro Bowl.

In 1977 Payton took home many awards and led the league as the leading scorer and was named as Most Valuable Player by Pro Football Writers of America and Associated Press. He broke many records that year included 273 rushing yards held by O. J. Simpson. He also held that record for 23 years and it is a notable one as he set it whilst playing against the Vikings with a fever of 101-degrees. The record was broken by Corey Dillon in October of 2000.

He won the Super Bowl XX in 1985 with the Chicago Bears and was inducted into the Hall of Fame in 1993. In November of 1999, Walter Payton passed away after a several month battle with rare liver disease. His legacy lives on through his cause to raise awareness for a great need of organ donation, the Walter Payton Man of the Year Award and the Walter Payton Award.

Personal Information

There was confusion over Payton's birthdate which was listed as July 25, 1954, when in fact it is birth year was actually 1953. He was born in Columbia, Mississippi and attended Columbia High School. He died at the age of 45 on November 1, 1999, in South Barrington, Illinois.

In 1976 he married Connie Norwood and the couple had two children together. When he announced he was suffering from liver disease in 1999 they set up the Walter and Connie foundation. The foundation advocates for the need for organ donation to save lives and is accredited with getting the message out across the nation. The foundation also gives toys to underprivileged children every Christmas and in 2002 his family set up the Walter Payton Cancer Fund.

NFL HALL OF FAME

Early Years
Not wanting to compete with his older brother that was on the football team Payton did not participate in the sport in his first years in high school. Instead, he was on the track team, sang in the school choir and played in the marching band. It was not until his brother graduated high school that Payton tried out for the football team. He excelled at the sport and was soon a successful high school running back earning statewide honors playing for Mississippi's all-state team.

He attended Jackson State University where he played with many other soon to be professional football players such as Jackie Slater, Robert Brazile, and Jerome Barkum. Payton was selected for the All-American Team and graduated in 1975 with a bachelor's degree in Communications.

NFL HALL OF FAME

Tom Brady

Career
Tom Brady was a late NFL selection in 2000 but has gone on to become known as "the biggest steal in NFL history". He won a Super Bowl in his first season to become the second quarterback in the league to do so. Brady has played for the Patriots in 10 Super Bowls and holds many of the league's records, trophies, and titles. He is also the oldest player in the competition to have won League MVP and Super Bowl MVP awards. In February 2019 he became the first player ever to have won 6 Super Bowls.

He has led the Patriots to become a formidable force that has now won the Super Bowl 3 years in a row. He is most definitely a candidate for the NFL Hall of Fame in the near future with his incredible Football career.

Tom Brady was drafted by the NFL in 2000 and was overall pick number 199 in round 6. He has played for the New England Patriots for 19 seasons not missing a game due to injury since 2008. He has been the starter quarterback at nearly every one of the New England Patriot games since he first took on the position.

Personal Information
Born in San Mateo, California in 1977 and shares his sporting fame with a great-uncle that played for Major League Baseball in 1884 through to 1885. He had a love of football and attended games with his father at Candlestick Park. His football hero was Joe Montana who he witnessed Joe Montana's famous throw to Dwight Clark that became known as "The Catch".

At a football camp, he attended he was coached by Tony Graziani who went on to become NFL/AFL quarterback for the Los Angeles Avengers.

Tom Brady was inducted into the Junipero Serra High School Hall of Fame in 2003. In 2012 Tom revisited his old high school to find that they had named the football stadium "Brady Family Stadium".

He is not only a football star but also has a line of health/organic foods which was launched after his sport/fitness website TB12Sports.com. Brady has also done a few voice overs for popular animated TV series such as The Simpsons and Family Guy. He has also done cameo appearances in the movies Ted 2 and Entourage Movie (he also appeared in an episode of the TV series).

Early Years
In high school, Brady played many sports including basketball, baseball and football. His football career began with him playing for the Padres Junior Varsity team. He was the backup quarterback not being good enough back then to start. He eventually became the starting quarterback when the current one was injured and then held the position until he graduated.

Tom was also an excellent baseball player and was drafted by the Montreal Expos in the 18th round of the 1995 MLB draft. But his love of football drove him forward and he was recruited by Bill Harris to play for Michigan University in 1995.

NFL HALL OF FAME

Joe Montana

Career

Joe Montana is a former 49ers quarterback that was nicknamed the "Comeback Kid" or "Joe Cool". He played in the NFL from 1979 through to 1994 where he ended his pro football career playing for the Kansas City Chiefs.

He was inducted into the Hall of Fame in 2000 he became the first player ever to be named as the Super Bowls most Valuable Player. He still holds the all-time highest records for a passer rating of 127.8 and the most passes without inception in a Super Bowl which is 122 in 4 games.

He went on to break a few NFL records and win many NFL Titles throughout this legendary career including the NFL 75th Anniversary All-Time Team, NFL 1980s All-Decade Team to name but a few.

Joe was traded to the Kansas City Chiefs in 1993 and led the team to its first AFC Championship game in January of 1994 his last football season. His number 16 jersey was retired by the 49ers and his career highlights include that of what became known as "The Catch" which was the winning touchdown pass of the 1981 NFC Championship game the 49ers played against the Dallas. In the Super Bowl XXIII, his winning 92-yard drive will always be remembered in the 49ers game against the Bengals.

He was named by ESPN as the 25th greatest athlete of the 20th century in 1999 along with being ranked 3rd on The Sporting News "Football's 100 Greatest Players" list. Sports Illustrated labeled him the number-one clutch quarterback of all time in 2006.

Montana is well known for his comeback victories having racked up a total of 31 with him as a quarterback. Of those 26 were whilst he was playing for the 49ers and the rest during his time with the chiefs. He got the nickname "Joe Cool" for his ability to stay calm during tense key moments of the game.

Personal Information

Joe Clifford Montana Jr. was born in New Eagle, Pennsylvania on June 11, 1956. He attended Ringgold High School in Carroll, Pennsylvania.

At the age of 8, Joe started to play youth football encouraged to do so by his father who enlisted him as a 9-year-old so he would get into the league. Joe also had an interest in baseball as well as basketball which, as a child, was his most favored sport.

At Ringgold high school Joe played basketball, football and baseball helping the school to win the 1973 WPIAL Class AAA boys basketball championships. He was also named all-state-player for his part in this victory.

He married Kim Moses, who was his sweetheart from his hometown, in 1974 but was divorced three years

NFL HALL OF FAME

later. He married Cass Castillo in 1981 only to be divorced in 1984 and he was married to Jennifer Wallace in 1985 with whom he has four children, two daughters and two sons that all play football.

He has a bridge named after him, the Mingo Creek Viaduct which carries Pennsylvania Routh 43 over the creek. This route runs close to where he went to Ringgold high school.

Early Years
Montana was offered a basketball scholarship by North Carolina State University, but he turned down the offer as he considered NCSU on a promise that he could play both of his favorite sports which were football and basketball. But he took up the offer from Notre Dame as his football idol Terry Hanratty, a quarterback for the Pittsburg Steelers attended the establishment.

He only got to play at Notre Dame with the major football team during his sophomore years due to University rules at the time that prevented freshman from practicing or playing with the varsity team.

Joe Montana became a key player at Notre Dame especially under their new coach Dan Devine. He was drafted in the third round as overall pick number 82 in the 1979 NFL Draft by the 49ers.

NFL HALL OF FAME

Reggie White

Career

Reggie White was a defensive end who started his pro football career playing for the USFL (United States Football Leagues) and the Memphis Showboats for two seasons (1985 to 1985). He was drafted to the NFL in the supplemental draft in 1984 during the first round as overall pick number 4.

He began his NFL pro football career playing for the Philadelphia Eagles from 1985 through to 1992 before joining the Green Bay Packers for from 1993 to 1998. In 2000 he joined the Carolina Panthers.

In 1985 the USFL collapsed and Reggie White was drafted into the NFL by the Eagles where he was reported to have taken a pay cut. He had joined the Eagles after the 1985 season began as an unknown entity. But by his first game with the Eagles, his name was quite well known due to making two-and-a-half sacks and ten tackles. By the end of his first season with the Eagles White received the title of NFC defensive rookie of the year.

In his 121 games he played for the Eagles through eight seasons he racked up 124 sacks to take the team record of Eagles all-time sack leader, Eagles regular-season sack record. He also became the only player in the NFL to rack up 20 or more sacks in only 12 games. In 1987 he set yet another NFL sacks record for averaging most sacks per game and by the end of his time with the Eagles, he had accumulated more sacks than he had played games. ESPN Sportsnation voted him the greatest player in the history of the Eagles franchise.

Upon becoming a free agent in 1993 he was signed by the Green Bay Packers where he played for six seasons. He became the all-time sacks leader of the time for the Packers with another 68.5 sacks to his career stats. He was instrumental in the Packer winning the Super Bowl XXXI with is game ending sack.

He was named the NFL Defensive Player of the Year twice the last being in 1998 and he retired the following year (1999).

In 2000 he came out of his one-year retirement to join the Carolina Panthers where he started all 16 games of the season. He retired at the end of the season and four years later on December 26, 2004, he died of arrhythmia at the age of 43.

Reggie White was inducted into the Hall of Fame in 2006.

Personal Information

Reginald Howard White was born on December 19, 1961, in Chattanooga, Tennessee.

He attended Howard high school in Chattanooga where he played for the high school football team and coach Robert Pulliam. During his senior year of playing with the Hustlin Tigers, he managed 140 tackles

NFL HALL OF FAME

of which 80 were solo and 10 sacks. He went on to receive All-American honors and was rated as the number one recruit by the Knoxville New Sentinel for Tennessee.

From the age of 12, Reggie wanted to become both a minister and a football player. Both of which he achieved in his lifetime. During his university years, he was interested in becoming an evangelist and was involved with the Fellowship of Christian Athletes.

The Reggie White Sleep Disorders Research and Education was found by his wife Sarah along with the Sleep Wellness Institute after his death. The institute is dedicated to people who have various types of sleep disorders.

Early Years
From 1980 to 1983 Reggie played college football for the University of Tennessee in which he had become the starting line backer by his freshman year. The Andy Spiva award was given to him that year for the most improved player.

By the end of his 1981 season, Reggie took the title of the Best Defensive Player and was the Football News named him to the Sophomore All-American team.

For his various college records that he held he was inducted into the College Football Hall of Fame.

NFL HALL OF FAME

Peyton Manning

Career

Peyton Manning has an impressive football career which spanned across 18 seasons after being drafted by the NFL as the first pick of the first round in 1998. He played most of his football career in the League for the Indianapolis Colts until 2011. He joined the Denver Broncos for 4 seasons from 2012 through to 2015.

With his many career highlights and achievements, he is a contender for the NFL Hall of Fame. He took the Colts from a struggling team to formidable playoff contenders leading them to 1 Super Bowl, 8 Division championships and 2 AFC championships.

In 2011 Manning missed the entire NFL season due to neck surgery after which he was released by the Indianapolis Colts to play for the Denver Broncos. His neck surgery did not slow him down as the Broncos reached the top of their division each year from 2011 to 2015 under his leadership. In 2015 he ended his career on a high note as the Broncos won the Super Bowl 50.

Manning holds NFL records for touchdown passes – 539, 14 Pro Bowl appearances and 5 AP MVP awards to name but a few of his achievements. When he won the Super Bowl 50, he became the oldest NFL Player to have achieved this at the age of 39. This has since been beaten by Tom Brady at the age of 41.

He retired from football on October 7, 2017, after having won a total of 9 ESPY Awards. He has a bronze statue outside the Lucas Oil Stadium and was inducted into the Indianapolis Colts Ring of Honor. He was the first of the Colts players to have his jersey retired.

Personal Information

Peyton Manning was born in New Orleans, Louisiana in on March 24, 1976. He attended New Orleans (LA) Isidore Newman Highschool.

After starting his NFL career he started "the Peyback Foundation" which helps disadvantaged kids in the Indiana, Louisiana, and Tennessee areas. For his charitable contributions and efforts, he won the Samuel S. Beard Award. The award is given to individuals under the age of 35 for the Greatest Public service by an individual. He and his wife are known for their support of children in need and as such St. Vincent Hospital in Indianapolis renamed its children ward after him.

Early Years

In high school (1993) he was named the Gatorade Circle of Champions National Player of the Year. He was also named the Columbus, Ohio, Touchdown Club Nation Offensive Player of the year.

As he led his high school team in many a victory, he soon became one of the most sought-after players by college recruits. He was made offers by over 60 colleges and selected to join the University of Tennessee. As with his high school football achievements he went on to accumulate many University ones.

In 2016 he was inducted into the Tennessee Athletics Hall of fame and named the Tennessean of the Year by the Tennessee Sports Hall of fame that same year. In 2017 he was elected to the College Football Hall of Fame as was his father Archie in his day. They are the first father and son to have been inducted.

NFL HALL OF FAME

Don Hutson

Career
Don Hutson was a split end for the Green Bay Packers throughout his entire pro football career which lasted eleven years. The Packers took four NFL Championships with Hutson on their team in which they had three victories in 1936, 1939 and 1944.

During his professional career, he held NFL records in for receiving touchdowns through nine seasons and receiving yards in seven seasons. In 1940 his talent as a safety on defense gave him the NFL lead in interceptions. He became an eight-time All-Pro selection and a four-time All-Star as well as being awarded the NFL MVP and Joe F. Carr trophy twice.

Considered as the first modern receiver of the NFL he was instrumental in quite a few of the modern pass routes which are still incorporated by the NFL. He was the most influential receiver of his era in the NFL and held a lot of the major receiving records for his career yards, touchdowns and receptions.

Don Hutson wore the number 14 jersey for the Green Bay Packers, and it was the first jersey to be retired by the team. He was inducted into the College Hall of Fame as a charter member and into the Pro Football Hall of Fame in 1963. At the National Football League 75th Anniversary in 1994, he was selected for the All-Time Team to be recognized as one of the greatest players in the first 75-year history of the NFL.

Don Hutson retired as an NFL player after the 1945 season and went on to be an assistant coach to the Green Bay Packers until 1948. He died at the age of 84 on June 26, 1997.

Personal Information
Donald Montgomery Hudson was born in Pine Bluff, Arkansas on January 31, 1913. He attended Pine Bluff high school in Alabama. He attributes his speed and agility to having played with snakes whilst a member of the boy scouts.

During high school, he played baseball for the town team and as a senior, he was an all-state basketball player. His favorite sport during school was basketball and said that he liked to watch football and play basketball. During his high school year, he only played football for a total of one year.

Early Years
Hutson attended the University of Alabama where he played football for the Alabama Crimson Tide team. The tides were undefeated in 1934 and were named by Morgan Blake (a sports writer of the time) as the best team he had ever seen. Hutson was known for his inventive maneuvering and faked moves.

Six different organizations recognized Hutson as a first-team All-American. He was awarded the Heisman Trophy by the National Football Foundation in 1934.

NFL HALL OF FAME

When he graduated from Alabama, he was not that interested in playing for the NFL as it was not quite established back them especially in the south. But he ended up signing with both the Green Bay Packers and the Brooklyn Dodgers. The NFL decided that since the signing of the Green Bay Pacers contract was with an earlier date that Hutson would have to play with them. During this era, the NFL had yet to establish the draft as such players had autonomy to sign with whichever team they chose.

Hutson first catches as a professional player came from the first play from scrimmage in a game against the Chicago Bears during the second half of the 1935 season. His catch was the first and only score of the game which won it 7-0 for the Packers. He led the league in touchdowns during his rookie season and there after for another consecutive three seasons.

Huston went on to lead the league in many records and is credited for many of the unique game plays still used by the NFL. He announced his retirement from playing football in 1943 (February) as he had a chest injury which was not clearing up. But as the season started, he changed his mind and played the season through. In this season he went on to score 11 touchdowns, caught 47 passes for 776 yards another League record for that season.

In 1942 Huston held the league of 17 touchdown receptions in a single season which stood for 42 years before it was broken. He still holds the record for the highest career average touchdowns per game for a receiver (0.85). He never once missed a game because of an injury in his entire 11-year career. His famous chair route pass is still in use with the NFL today.

NFL HALL OF FAME

Dick Butkus

Career

Richard (Dick) Butkus was a linebacker for the Chicago Bears from 1965 to 1973. He was Drafted to the NFL in round one as the third pick in 1965 and to the AFL in round two as the ninth pick of the second round in the same year.

During his career, he had many career highlights, awards and was regarded as one of the most formidable linebackers in pro football history. Born in Chicago Illinois he stayed true to his home state where he played football throughout his career.

The NFL Network named Butkus the most feared tackler of all time in 2009 and was said to be "a well-conditioned animal, and that every time he hit you, he tried to put you in the cemetery, not the hospital" by Deacon Jones.

To this day he considered being "the gold standard by which other middle linebackers are measured" and is credited to defining the middle linebacker position. His no. 15 jersey was retired by the Bears and he was inducted into the Hall of Fame in 1979.

During his career, he recovered 227 fumbles, intercepted 22 passes and caused many a fumble with his potent tackles. He was both feared and admired on the field by his opponents.

In 1973 Butkus's knee injury caused him to cut the season short after only 9 games in. His knee injury had been with him for years and he had been warned by orthopedic surgeon years before that he should not be playing. He was finally forced to give in and retire at the age of 31 in May of 1974.

Personal Information

Dick Butkus (Richard Marvin) was born in Chicago, Illinois on December 9, 1942. He attended Vocational High School.

He played linebacker, punter, and fullback for his high school football team as well as a placekicker. His preference was as a linebacker as he was good at the position accounting for 70 percent of the team's tackles.

The Chicago Sun-Times honored him as Chicago's high school player of the year in 1959 making him the first to receive such an honor. Colleges from all over tried to recruit him even though he could not play as much during his senior year due to injuries.

Early Years

From 1962 to 1964 Butkus played for the Illinois Fighting Illini football team of the University of Illinois. Here he played the positions of linebacker and center where the Associated Press he named as the 1962 All-Big Ten Conference football team. The United Press International named him as the second-team center in the same year.

He led the Illini to win the 1964 Rose bowl over the Washington he was awarded the Chicago Tribune Silver Football for being the Big Ten's most valuable player. It was a unanimous choice for his to be the center for the College Football All-American Team in 1963. This led him to be awarded first-team honors which he got from all seven selectors.

NFL HALL OF FAME

Brett Favre

Career

Brett Favre spent most of his career with the Green Bay Packers after spending his first NFL season with the Atlanta Falcons in 1991. He was drafted by the Atlanta Falcons as Pick number 33 of Round 2 in the 1991 NFL draft. He was a backup quarterback for the Falcons before being traded to the Packers in the first round of the 1992 draft.

He played for Green Bay for 16 years before he was traded to the Jet with whom he played for the 2008 season. Favre spent his final 2 football season playing for the Vikings. During his long football career he has accumulated many club and NFL records, titles and awards. Including that of the only NFL player to have won 3 consecutive Associated Press NFL Most Valuable Player Award (1995 – 1997).

Upon his retirement he was the NFL's record holder for most career passing touchdowns, most times sacked, most fumbles, most career interceptions thrown and most consecutive starts by a player.

In 2016 Brett Favre was inducted into the Pro Football Hall of Fame.

Personal Information

Born in Gulfport, Mississippi on the 10th October 1969 where he was raised in a small town called Kiln. His parents were both teachers and he was one of four children.

He attended Hancock North Central High School where he was an avid sports player enjoying both football and baseball. He earned 5 varsity letters for playing baseball. In football he played a few positions during high school such as quarterback, strong safety, placekicker, punter and quarterback. His father was the head coach of his high school football team the Hawks.

Early Years

Favre joined the University of Southern Mississippi on a football scholarship leading the Golden Eagles a few game winning victories during his varsity football career.

In 1990 he was involved in a near fatal car accident where he flipped his car going around a bend. He was back on the football field 6 weeks later to lead the Southern Mississippi to a victory over Alabama.

TEAMS OF THE NFL

BUFFALO BILLS

The Buffalo Bills started as a charter team for the America Football League (AFL) in 1960. Buster Ramsey was the head coach for the team during this period. Whilst a member of the AFL the team won two championship titles one in 1964 and again the following year in 1965.

The Bills became part of the NFL with the AFL/NFL merger in 1970 becoming the second city represented team after the Buffalo All-Americans that folded in 1929. The Buffalo Bills are a member club that plays for the AFC division of the NFL as part of the East division. The team was owned by Ralph Wilson from its inception until he died at age 95 in 2014. It was in this year that upon approval from other NFL team owners that Kim and Terry Pegula bought the Bills franchise from Wilson's estate.

They have been one of the only NFL teams to have lost four consecutive Super Bowl games (1991, 1992, 1993, 1994). They are also the only team to have won four conference championship games in a row (same years as they lost the Super Bowl). They are also the only NFL team that had an "active playoff drought" lasting over a decade. Their active playoff drought lasted from 1999 to 2017 making them the last of the league's teams to compete in a playoff game in the 21st century.

The Bills had a near collapse in the 1980s right through to the middle of the 90s. But due to some high draft picks and the folding of the United States Football League the Bills were able to rebuild their team to bounce back with a fighting chance. In 1991 they went on to win four back to back AFC Championships making it to the Super Bowl four years in a row. Unfortunately, they were not able to claim a Super Bowl victory in these years.

For seventeen years the Bills did not secure a position in the playoffs until they got a wildcard berth in 2017. They lost their playoff game 3 – 10 to the Jacksonville Jaguars but it ended one of the longest playoff droughts for the team making NFL history.

In their 49th franchise season in the NFL, the team ended the season with 6 wins and 10 losses ending in AFC East 3rd position and 13th in their division without having qualified for the 2018 playoffs. They failed to improve on their 2017 9-7 record in 2018 after having lost to Miami Dolphins 21 -17. The next week they played against the New York Jets losing 27 – 23 eliminating them from playoff contention which has not happened to the Bills since 2016.

The 2018 Bills season was the 59th official season of the Bills team, the 4th season under the new ownership of Kim and Terry Pegula and the second season under the new management of Brandon Beane and Head coach Sean McDermott. After the 2017/18 season ended Russ Brandon, the team president resigned from Pegula Sports and Entertainment. In his statement to the press announcing his retirement, he told the press that he had fulfilled his twenty-year duty to both the Sabres and Bills.

Buffalo Bills Franchise Encyclopedia

Seasons: 60 (1960 to 2019)

Record (W-L-T): 415-477-8

Playoff Record: 14-16

Super Bowls Won: 0 (4 Appearances)

Championships Won*: 2

All-time Passing Leader: Jim Kelly 2,874/4,779, 35,467 yds, 237 TD

All-time Rushing Leader: Thurman Thomas 2,849 att, 11,938 yds, 65 TD

All-time Receiving Leader: Andre Reed 941 rec, 13,095 yds, 86 TD

All-time Scoring Leader: Steve Christie 1,011 points

All-time AV Leader: Bruce Smith 194 AV

Winningest Coach: Marv Levy 112-70-0

TEAMS OF THE NFL

MIAMI DOLPHINS

The Miami Dolphins are Florida's oldest professional sports team being formed in 1966 by Joe Robbie (an attorney/politician) and actor-comedian Danny Thomas. The team became a member of the AFL when they started and joined the NFL with the merger in 1970. The Dolphins play for the AFC Eastern Division of the league and are the only team out of the four that was not a charter member of the AFL.

Before the inception of the Miami Dolphins, the region had not been represented by a professional football team since the folding of the Miami Seahawks in 1946. The Dolphins trained and practiced at the Saint Andrews private boys' school for their first few years as a team. The Miami Orange Bowl was their home game stadium from 1966 to 1986. It was also the home stadium for the Miami Hurricanes college football team during their regular season. In 1987 the Hard Rock Stadium in Miami Gardens, Florida was opened and now hosts the Dolphins home games.

They have won 13 AFC Division Championships, have made 23 Playoff appearances, appeared in 5 Super Bowls of which they won 2 (Super Bowl VII and Super Bowl VIII). Their first Super Bowl appearance (Super Bowl VI) they lost 24 – 3 to the Dallas Cowboys. The next year they made they once again made it to the Super Bowl and won against the Washington Redskins. This victory came after they had completed a perfect season where they won all 14 of their regular season games. They became the fifth NFL team in the league's history to accomplish this.

They went on to become the first team of the NFL to make it through to three consecutive Super Bowl Championships. Their Super Bowl VII championship victory made them the second team in the league's history to win two consecutive championship games. The Dolphins next Championship appearance was the Super Bowl XVII where they lost to their former rivals the Washington Redskins. They were once again defeated by the San Francisco 49ers in the Super Bowl XIX game.

In 1970 former football Defensive Back and former Baltimore Colts Head Coach, Don Shula became the Head Coach for the Dolphins. Having played for teams such as the Cleveland Browns, Baltimore Colts and Washington Redskins he retired from playing in 1957. In 1960 he took a position as Defensive Co-Ordinator for the Detroit Lions before becoming the Head Coach for the Baltimore Colts in 1963. In 1993 Shula was named as the Sportsman of the Year by Sports Illustrated. He is known as one of the most successful coaches in the history of football shaving had only two losing seasons in his 33-year Head Coach career in the NFL. He has taken his teams to six Super Bowls breaking records and making history along the way.

The Miami Dolphins became a formidable force under the leadership of Don Shula and the rise of Dan Marino who broke many an NFL passing record. The 1980s and 1990s saw an exciting rivalry between the Dolphins and the Buffalo Bills, who they beat in every division game during the 1970s. With the emergence of quarterbacks such as Tom Brady and the retirement of Shula and Marino, the Dolphins have struggled to regain their seat in the championship.

Miami Dolphins Franchise Encyclopedia

Seasons: 54 (1966 to 2019)

Record (W-L-T): 452-360-4

Playoff Record: 20-21

Super Bowls Won: 2 (5 Appearances)

Championships Won*: 2

All-time Passing Leader: Dan Marino 4,967/8,358, 61,361 yds, 420 TD

All-time Rushing Leader: Larry Csonka 1,506 att, 6,737 yds, 53 TD

All-time Receiving Leader: Mark Duper 511 rec, 8,869 yds, 59 TD

All-time Scoring Leader: Olindo Mare 1,048 points

All-time AV Leader: Dan Marino 216 AV

Winningest Coach: Don Shula 257-133-2

TEAMS OF THE NFL

NEW ENGLAND PATRIOTS

Billy Sullivan, a Boston Business Executive, was awarded the eighth (which was also the final) AFL franchise in 1959. The team was first named the Boston Patriots was chosen from selections of names submitted by the local Bostonians invited to help choose their teams name. "Pat Patriot" became the Patriots logo and was drawn by Phil Bissell who worked for The Boston Globe.

The team played under the name of the Boston Patriots from 1960 through to 1970. They did not have a dedicated home field but played their games at various stadiums in Boston including Nickerson Field (1960 – 1962), Fenway Park (1963 – 1968), Alumni Stadium (1969), Harvard Stadium (1970).

During their early years, the Patriots struggled to gain a position within the AFL making it to only one of the leagues Championships games in 1963. They were defeated 51 – 10 by the San Diego Chargers and did not make another post-season AFL game.

In 1970 they joined the National Football League in the merge with the AFL and were placed in the East Division of the American Football Conference (AFC) division. The Patriots were moved to the Foxboro Stadium in Foxborough, Massachusetts, which was to become their new home game field in 1971. Because of the move, the team announced a name change to the "Bay State Patriots" but the NFL rejected it. Instead, the name was changed to New England Patriots.

It took the Patriots thirteen years from their first AFL Championship game to earn a place in another championship game. In 1976 their hard work earned them a birth as a wild card team in the Playoffs and they won the AFC Championships in 1978.

Boston/New England Patriots Franchise Encyclopedia

Seasons: 60 (1960 to 2019)

Record (W-L-T): 500-391-9

Playoff Record: 37-20

Super Bowls Won: 6 (11 Appearances)

Championships Won*: 6

All-time Passing Leader: Tom Brady 6,004/9,375, 70,514 yds, 517 TD

All-time Rushing Leader: Sam Cunningham 1,385 att, 5,453 yds, 43 TD

All-time Receiving Leader: Stanley Morgan 534 rec, 10,352 yds, 67 TD

All-time Scoring Leader: Stephen Gostkowski 1,743 points

All-time AV Leader: Tom Brady 269 AV

Winningest Coach: Bill Belichick 225-79-0

The 1970s saw the Patriots rise in strength through to the early 1980s where they made it through the Playoffs to the Super Bowl XX in 1985. Although they lost to the Chicago Bears 46 – 10 they returned to the Playoffs in 1986 but did not make it through to the Championship game.

The following eight years were rough on the team as they did not make the playoffs and went 1 -15 in the 1990 season. Over the next fourteen years, the team changed ownership four times after being sold from the Sullivan family. In 1988 the team was first sold to Victor Kiam who sold it to James Orthwein who brought about a major change to the team including the new team uniform color to blue and silver. He also oversaw the development of the new team logo and had intended to move the team to St. Louis, Missouri where it would be renamed the St. Louis Stallions. Before he uprooted the team, he sold it to Robert Kraft of the Kraft Group in 1994.

Under the ownership of Kraft, the team went from strength to strength selling out every home game. Coached by Bill Parcells the team appeared in two Playoff games and the Super Bowl XXXI which they lost to the Green Bay Packers 35 – 21. Parcells successor Pete Carroll saw the team reach the playoffs in both 1997 and 1998. In 2000 Bill Belichick was hired as head coach for the Patriots after Carroll's dismissal in 1999.

Since 2000 the Patriots have become one of the most successful teams in the history of the NFL. Under their Head Coach Belichick and the emergence of quarterback Tom Brady the team has not has a losing season since 2001. Over eighteen seasons they have won six AFC titles setting a whole lot of new NFL records.

TEAMS OF THE NFL

NEW YORK JETS

The New York Jets were formed in 1959 as the Titans of New York, a charter member of the American Football League. Their first season was in 1960 and their home field was the Polo Grounds from 1960 through to 1963. Their current home field is the MetLife Stadium which they share with the New York Giants having moved there in 2010.

Harry Wismer was granted the AFL franchise he named Titans of New York in 1959 securing the run-down Polo Grounds as the team's home field. The team suffered financially in its first three years of inception forcing the AFL to finally take over its costs until the end of the 1962 season.

The team was saved from financial ruin by Sonny Werblin who headed a five-man syndicate that bought the team. After purchase, the team was renamed the New York Jets as they were moved to a new stadium near LaGuardia Airport – Shea Stadium. Werblin shook up the team's management and hired Weeb Ewbank as the manager and head coach.

With new management in place, a new stadium and more financial stability the Jets were taken to new heights as quarterback Joe Namath led the team to victory over the Baltimore Colts in Super Bowl III. Under new ownership, management and head coach the team secured their position in professional football and the AFL.

After the NFL and AFL merged the Jets once again started to decline especially after their star quarterback Joe Namath sustained injuries that severely affected his game and career giving him only three successful post-merge seasons with the Jets. It was not until the 1980s that they bounced back into the limelight with the popular "New York Sack Exchange" emergence and appeared in the 1982 AFC Championship Game.

In 1968 after a disagreement with his partners as to the running of the team Werblin agreed to be bought out by his partners. Leon Hess became the team's major stakeholder in 1973 and by 1985 he had become the sole owner of the Jets after buying out the remaining partners. After a string of unsuccessful seasons and a few head coaches under the team's belt, he eventually hired Bill Parcells with a dream of getting his team to the Super Bowl but sadly passed away in 1999 before his dream transpired.

The Jets have had a major turn over of head coaches through their history with Bill Parcells being the first to lead the team to an AFC Championship game in 1998 before stepping down in 1999. With a new owner, Woody Johnson (bought the team in 2000) the team went through three head coaches but managed to get to the playoffs five times.

The Jets have only reached the championship game once in 1968 but they have appeared in thirteen playoff games since they started their first season in 1960. In 2015 Todd Bowles, the former Defensive Co-Ordinator for the Arizona Cardinals was appointed Head Coach. After the Jets finished the 2018 season 4 – 12 it was announced that Todd Bowls would no longer be coaching the Jets.

New York Jets Franchise Encyclopedia

Seasons: 60 (1960 to 2019)

Record (W-L-T): 401-491-8

Playoff Record: 12-13

Super Bowls Won: 1 (1 Appearance)

Championships Won*: 1

All-time Passing Leader: Joe Namath 1,836/3,655, 27,057 yds, 170 TD

All-time Rushing Leader: Curtis Martin 2,560 att, 10,302 yds, 58 TD

All-time Receiving Leader: Don Maynard 627 rec, 11,732 yds, 88 TD

All-time Scoring Leader: Pat Leahy 1,470 points

All-time AV Leader: Don Maynard 132 AV

Winningest Coach: Weeb Ewbank 71-77-6

TEAMS OF THE NFL

BALTIMORE RAVENS

The original Baltimore Colts NFL team from 1953 to 1983 having their home stadium at Memorial Stadium. The city of Indianapolis, India made an offer on Colts Franchise and after a Battle with the City of Baltimore were relocated to Indianapolis in March of 1984. It was not until 1986 that Baltimore established a new football team the Baltimore Ravens originally the Cleveland Browns. After a lot of controversy with the Browns move from Cleveland it was agreed that all the Browns franchise records and everything pertaining to the team such as the uniforms, colors, club records and Pro Football Hall of Fame members, etc. Not all players or staff connected with the Browns relocated with the team.

For their first two seasons, the Ravens played at Baltimore's Memorial Stadium as their home fields. This was the same stadium that had been used by the previous two Baltimore teams the Baltimore Stallions and the Baltimore Colts. In 1998 the Ravens moved into their new home stadium M&T Bank Stadium located next to Camden Yards in Baltimore.

Ted Marchibroda was hired as head coach by owner Art Modell after the relocation. The Ravens won the first opening game in 1996 but ended the season 4 -12 despite the great efforts of Michael Jackson the Ravens receiver who led the league with 14 touchdown catches that season.

In 1998 the Colts returned to Baltimore to battle the Ravens on their home field. It was the first time in fifteen years that the Colts had been back in Baltimore. They were not received too well and the Ravens fans were delighted with their 38 – 31 victory over the Colts.

Brian Billick became the Ravens new head coach after the team had three consecutive losing seasons under Marchibroda. At the same time, Tony Banks former St. Louis Rams quarterback moved to the Ravens. Along with Qadry Ismail, former New Orleans Saints receiver had the best seasons with Qadry posting a 1000-yard season. Banks had the best season of his career making an 8:12 pass ratios with seventeen touchdowns making the initially struggling Ravens finish the season with an 8 – 8 records.

Art Modell was forced by the NFL to sell 49% of his team's shares due to financial hardships. These shares were bought by Steve Bisciotti, an American Business Executive and founder of Aerotek. In 2004 Bisciotti was given approval by the NFL to buy Models remaining 51% shares in the team.

Although they started off strong in the 2000 regular season the team struggled mid-season but managed to make it to the Playoffs for the first time. Filled with new-found confidence the Ravens went on to beat Oakland Raiders 24 – 10 in the AFC Championship game. Their next stop was Tampa to play against the New York Giants for the Super Bowl XXXV. This had already been a remarkable year for the Ravens as their strong defense broke two of the NFL records.

The Ravens excellent defense forced five turnovers and recorded four sacks. The Giants only score that game was made by a kickoff return to touchdown by Ron Dixon. The Ravens won their first Championship game with a 34 – 7 victory over the Giants. Their Super Bowl win made them the third wild card team to win the title.

They have won two Conference Championships, five Division Championships, appeared in eleven Playoffs and won two Super Bowl Championships (Super Bowl XXXV in 2000 and Super Bowl XLVII in 2012). The Baltimore Ravens first played AFC Central from 1996 to 2000 and currently play AFC North since 2000 in the NFL.

Baltimore Ravens Franchise Encyclopedia

Seasons: 24 (1996 to 2019)

Record (W-L-T): 200-167-1

Playoff Record: 15-9

Super Bowls Won: 2 (2 Appearances)

Championships Won*: 2

All-time Passing Leader: Joe Flacco 3,499/5,670, 38,245 yds, 212 TD

All-time Rushing Leader: Jamal Lewis 1,822 att, 7,801 yds, 45 TD

All-time Receiving Leader: Derrick Mason 471 rec, 5,777 yds, 29 TD

All-time Scoring Leader: Matt Stover 1,464 points

All-time AV Leader: Ray Lewis 221 AV

Winningest Coach: John Harbaugh 104-72-0

TEAMS OF THE NFL

CINCINNATI BENGALS

Based in Cincinnati, Ohio the Cincinnati Bengals were established in 1967 having their first official season in 1968. Initially, a member of the AFL their original home field was Nippert Stadium up until 1969. With the NFL – AFL merger in 1970 the teams home became Riverfront Stadium up until 1999. In 2000 they took up residence at the Paul Brown Stadium and is where they currently play their home games.

Originally in the AFL West division, they became part of AFC Central in 1970 with the NFL merge up until 2001. They currently play in the AFC North division and have done since the 2002 season.

They were founded by Paul Brown who was the former Head Coach for the Cleveland Browns. The team is currently owned by his son Mike Brown who took over after his fathers' death in 1991. He became the majority shareholder of the team in 2011 after buying Austin Knowlton's shares from the family estate.

Both the 1990s and the 2000s have been a struggle for the Bengals who had not made any playoffs winning records since the 1990 season. A struggle that would last fourteen years with the team going through several head coaches and their now owner Mike Brown being dubbed one of the worst team owners of any American professional sports.

The appointment of Head Coach Marvin Lewis in the mid-2000s saw a turnaround in the team as they won their first division title in over ten years. In 2011 they acquired quarterback Andy Dalton who led the team to make the Playoffs every season from then up until 2016. However since 1990 they Bengals have not won a Playoff game and they are one of twelve NFL teams that have not won a Super Bowl and one of eight to have appeared in at least one Super Bowl game.

Marvin Lewis took over as the Bengals Head Coach from Dick LeBeau in 2003. During the team's years, they have won no Super Bowls, two AFC Conference Championships (1981 and 1988), nine Division Championships and appeared in fourteen Playoffs. They have made it to two Super Bowl Games (XVI and XXIII).

The Bengals have many interesting factors surrounding them like their mascot a Bengal tiger named Who Dey and their cheerleading squad the Cincinnati Ben-Gals. The Ben-Gals are famous for having the oldest cheerleading in an NFL Cheerleading squad. Laura Vikmanis a dietician, dancer, and personal trainer. She joined the Ben-Gals in 2009 at the age of 40 and co-authored the book "It's Not About the Pom-Poms".

Since 2015 the team has had three straight losing seasons ending the 2018 season with their final record 6 – 10 and talk of their current Head Coach Marvin Lewis parting ways with the Bengals.

Cincinnati Bengals Franchise Encyclopedia

Seasons: 52 (1968 to 2019)

Record (W-L-T): 357-427-4

Playoff Record: 5-14

Super Bowls Won: 0 (2 Appearances)

Championships Won*: 0

All-time Passing Leader: Ken Anderson 2,654/4,475, 32,838 yds, 197 TD

All-time Rushing Leader: Corey Dillon 1,865 att, 8,061 yds, 45 TD

All-time Receiving Leader: Chad Johnson 751 rec, 10,783 yds, 66 TD

All-time Scoring Leader: Jim Breech 1,151 points

All-time AV Leader: Anthony Munoz 174 AV

Winningest Coach: Marvin Lewis 131-122-3

KEN ANDERSON

TEAMS OF THE NFL

CLEVELAND BROWNS

The Cleveland Browns were formed in 1945 by Arthur McBride with their first season in 1946 led by their coach Paul Brown. For their first three years, they played for the All-American Football Conference as part of the Western Division up until 1949. Their team has stood out in their unique orange, brown and white uniform colors with no logo on their helmets. They were a character member of the AAFC and a formidable team winning all four seasons championships with an impressive 47-4-3 record.

The AAFC folded in 1949 when the season ended, and the Browns joined the NFL in 1950. In that same year, they went on to win the NFL Championships. From 1945 through 1955 the Browns made it to each of their league's championships game making them the only team to ever accomplish this in the history of American professional sports.

From 1946 up until 1965 (the last time the one the NFL Championship) they had won eight (8) League Championships (4 for the AAFC and 4 with the NFL). They had made the playoffs fourteen (14) times. Between 1965 through to 1995 they made the playoffs another fourteen (14) but did not win any of the games to reach the championships.

Art Modell who bought the Browns in 1961 moved the Browns team to Baltimore where they became the Baltimore Ravens. But he no longer owned the intellectual property for the Browns as part of the agreement in moving the team. The team's name, colors, logo, etc. were kept in trust by the city of Cleveland with them regarded as suspended by the NFL.

In 1998 it was announced the Cleveland Browns would resume operations as an NFL Expansion team. But since officially rejoining the league in 1999 the Browns have not been able to re-establish themselves as the driving force they once were. Since 1999 the Browns have had a 16-year playoff drought which is the longest in the NFL history.

They have had only two winning seasons since their NFL return which were in 2002 (where they made the playoffs) and again in 2007. Since 1999 the team has had no stability as they have started over 30 different quarterbacks. Their win-loss records up to the end of the 2018 season now stand at 95-224-1 with the 2018 season ending in a 0 – 16.

Despite getting the number one draft pick in these last few years the Browns have not had much success. The team was re-started in 1999 by their new owner Al Lerner who sold the team to the Jimmy Haslam in 2012. Since then they have gone through four general managers and four head coaches. They have just completed the worst two-year stretch in their history under their current head coach Hue Jackson.

The team have only ever had two home fields upon which they have played, Cleveland Stadium is where they started in 1946 up until 1995. In 1999 under their new owner and being re-instated into the NFL the teams home field moved to the FirstEnergy Stadium where they currently play.

Cleveland Browns Franchise Encyclopedia

Seasons: 71 (1946 to 2019)

Record (W-L-T): 516-494-14

Playoff Record: 16-20

Super Bowls Won: 0 (0 Appearances)

Championships Won*: 8

All-time Passing Leader: Brian Sipe 1,944/3,439, 23,713 yds, 154 TD

All-time Rushing Leader: Jim Brown 2,359 att, 12,312 yds, 106 TD

All-time Receiving Leader: Ozzie Newsome 662 rec, 7,980 yds, 47 TD

All-time Scoring Leader: Lou Groza 1,608 points

All-time AV Leader: Clay Matthews 124 AV

Winningest Coach: Paul Brown 158-48-8

TEAMS OF THE NFL

PITTSBURG STEELERS

The Pittsburgh Steelers were found in Pittsburgh, Pennsylvania in 1933 as a member of the NFL starting in the Eastern Division. They played in the Eastern Division from 1933 to 1943. They went on to play in the Western Division for the 1944 season returning to the Eastern Division in 1945 through to 1949. After switching divisions a few more times they currently play in the AFC North Division which they have done since the 2002 season.

Before the 1970 NFL/AFL merger they Steelers were the oldest football team in their league to never have won a championship. Which is in direct contrast to their post-1970 merger status as being one of the most successful NFL franchises along with the New England Patriots.

The modern era Steelers have won six Super Bowl titles and have played in sixteen. They have hosted eleven Conference Championship Games which is more than any other team in the NFL ever has. They have made thirty-one Playoff's and have won 23 Divisional Championships.

The originally started out as the Pittsburgh Pirates from 1933 up until 1939 when their name was changed to the Pittsburgh Steelers. Between 1969 and 1961 their remarkable Defensive line became known as the "Steel Curtain".

The team was originally owned by Art Rooney and has remained in his family since with his grandson Art Rooney II currently the majority shareholder. After a few home fields changes, they were moved to the Heinz Field which was opened in 2001 and is their current home field. The Heinz Field replaced the Three Rivers Stadium which housed the Steelers home games for thirty-one years.

They are the oldest team in the AFC division of the NFL and are fondly called Steeler Nation by their widespread fan base. Since the 1970 merger, the Steelers have moved from strength to strength are now one of the only teams in the league not to have a season with losses of twelve or more since the NFL has expanded to a sixteen-game season.

The Steelers are said to have the most impressive fan base in the NFL. This is pretty apparent in that every home game the Steelers have played has been sold out and such has been the trend since the 1972 season.

The Steelers have had sixteen head coaches since their beginning with Chuck Noll holding the position for the longest term before retiring after 23 years with the team in 1991. The current head coach, Mike Tomlin, took over the position in the 2007 season. He has since led the team to a Super Bowl victory (XLIII), two Conference Championships, six Division Championships, and 8 Playoffs.

Pittsburgh Steelers Franchise Encyclopedia

Seasons: 87 (1933 to 2019)

Record (W-L-T): 623-544-21

Playoff Record: 36-25

Super Bowls Won: 6 (8 Appearances)

Championships Won*: 6

All-time Passing Leader:
Ben Roethlisberger 4,616/7,168, 56,194 yds, 363 TD

All-time Rushing Leader:
Franco Harris 2,881 att, 11,950 yds, 91 TD

All-time Receiving Leader:
Hines Ward 1,000 rec, 12,083 yds, 85 TD

All-time Scoring Leader:
Gary Anderson 1,343 points

All-time AV Leader:
Ben Roethlisberger 185 AV

Winningest Coach:
Chuck Noll 193-148-1

TEAMS OF THE NFL

HOUSTON TEXANS

The Houston Texans play their home field at the NRG Stadium which they have done since 2002. The team was formed in 1999 by owner Bob McNair until his death in 2018 where the ownership went to his wife, Janice, and son D. Cal McNair.

The Houston Texans are the youngest franchise of the NFL having played their first season in 2002 for the AFC South division. They are an NFL expansion team after the Houston Oilers were moved to Nashville Tennessee to become the Tennessee Titans in 1996.

Throughout the first half of the 2000s, the team struggled to gain success in the league until clinching their first playoff game in the 2011 season. The won the 2011 division championship and have since gone on to win another four AFC South championships (2012, 2015, 2016 and 2018) but are the only NFL franchise to have not yet appeared in a conference championship game.

The late 90s saw a few controversial teams move for the NFL including that of the Cleveland Browns to Baltimore in 96 and Bud Adams moving the Houston Oilers to Tennessee just a year later in 1997. As Cleveland was promised that the Browns would eventually be replaced as an expansion team the NFL looked at evening the teams out to 32 which would mean there was room for one more NFL expansion franchise.

After losing a bid for an NHL expansion team to Houston Bob McNair along founded Houston NFL holdings with partner Steve Patterson. With an association to Houston Livestock Show and Rodeo the pushed for a domed stadium in order to ensure a winning bid for the thirty-second NFL franchise. Houston was awarded the franchise in October of 1999 at a substantial cost of $700 million.

In the 2002 season, the new Houston Texans proudly joined the league playing their first game at the newly opened Reliant Stadium. The team won their first NFL Game with a victory over the Dallas Cowboys making them only expansion team since the Minnesota Vikings to win their opening game.

The Reliant Stadium was the first of the NFL Stadiums to have a retractable roof and the stadium's name was changed in 2002 to the NRG Stadium. The team had a bit of a battle during the early part of the 2000s until Gary Kubiak took over as head coach of the team in 2006. They finished that season with a .500 improving more each year since and nearly qualified for both the 2009 and 2010 NFL Playoffs.

Although they have not yet won an NFL Championship game, they have appeared in five playoffs and won five division championships. In 2014 the Texans signed former Penn State head coach Bill O'Brien.

During the 2018 season, the Texans owner Bob McNair died from skin cancer that November and his wife Janice McNair became the team's principal owner. They finished the 2018 season 11 – 5 having won another AFC Championships but losing 21 – 7 in the first round of the playoffs to the Indianapolis Colts.

Houston Texans Franchise Encyclopedia

Seasons: 18 (2002 to 2019)

Record (W-L-T): 121-151-0

Playoff Record: 3-5

Super Bowls Won: 0 (0 Appearances)

Championships Won*: 0

All-time Passing Leader: Matt Schaub 1,951/3,020, 23,221 yds, 124 TD

All-time Rushing Leader: Arian Foster 1,454 att, 6,472 yds, 54 TD

All-time Receiving Leader: Andre Johnson 1,012 rec, 13,597 yds, 64 TD

All-time Scoring Leader: Kris Brown 767 points

All-time AV Leader: Andre Johnson 120 AV

Winningest Coach: Gary Kubiak 61-64-0

ANDRE JOHNSON

TEAMS OF THE NFL

INDIANAPOLIS COLTS

The Indianapolis Colts that compete as a member club for the NFL Their current home field is the Lucas Oil Stadium based in the Indianapolis, Indiana. They are currently affiliated with the AFC South division where they have been since 2002.

Originally the Baltimore Colts that were formed in 1953 and have been a member club of the NFL since their beginning. With the 1970 merger, they became one of the three NFL teams to join the AFC. As the Baltimore Colts, the team won three NFL Championship games (1958, 1959 and 1968), appeared in the playoffs ten times and played in two Super Bowls.

On December 18, 1983, the Baltimore Colts played the Houston Oilers on their home field which was to be their last game as the Baltimore Colts. As the city could not offer an acceptable field upgrade proposal that suited both MLB and or the Colts franchise. James Irsay the team's owner had started negotiations for the team's relocation to better facilities. As the current stadium was not adequate and fan attendance had rapidly dropped off.

The choice of the team's relocation eventually came down to two cities which were Indianapolis and Phoenix. In order to lure the team to their city then Indianapolis Mayor Richard Lugar undertook an ambitious project in order to restore the city to a "Great American City" with the Hoosier Dome. The Dome was built for the NFL team and more than satisfied the NFL requirements as a home team stadium.

In the middle of the night on March 29, 1984 moving fans collected the Colts belongings and shipped them off to Maryland training complex. This was done as the city of Baltimore retaliated against the relocation of the Colts threatening Irsay with an eminent domain claim. In order to ensure that nothing of the team could be seized he had to move them out of Baltimore as fast as he could. By midday of the 29th March 1984, there was nothing left for the city of Baltimore to seize.

It was not until March of 1986 and a lot of legal battles in between did the city of Baltimore and the Colts come to a settlement agreement. The Colts would endorse a new NFL team for Baltimore and all the legal charges against them were dropped.

Before their move to Indianapolis and name change, the Colts were struggling. This struggle continued through to 1986 when head coach Rod Dowhower was fired after the teams only managed eight wins in two seasons. Dowhower was replaced by Ron Meyer and due to a trade during the 1987 season, the team acquired Erick Dickerson. With their new running back and head coach they went on to win the AFC East championship and as such advanced to the postseason. This was the first time they had made it this far as the Indianapolis Colts.

After a battle for the team's ownership with his stepmother upon the death of his father in 1997 Jim Irsay became the youngest NFL franchise owner at the age of 37. He promptly fired the head coach at the time which was Lindy Infante and hired Bill Polian as the general manager of the team. Bill hired Jim Mora as the team's head coach who in turn drafted the Peyton Manning who went on to be one of the greatest quarterbacks of all time.

It was the start of the Colts drive to success as they continued to draft top-notch players. Since then the team has had a few head coach changes but once again gained ground.

As the Indianapolis Colts, they have won one Super Bowl (XLI), two AFC and appeared in the Playoffs eighteen times.

Baltimore/Indianapolis Colts Franchise Encyclopedia

Seasons: 67 (1953 to 2019)

Record (W-L-T): 516-459-7

Playoff Record: 23-24

Super Bowls Won: 2 (4 Appearances)

Championships Won*: 4

All-time Passing Leader: Peyton Manning 4,682/7,210, 54,828 yds, 399 TD

All-time Rushing Leader: Edgerrin James 2,188 att, 9,226 yds, 64 TD

All-time Receiving Leader: Marvin Harrison 1,102 rec, 14,580 yds, 128 TD

All-time Scoring Leader: Adam Vinatieri 1,442 points

All-time AV Leader: Peyton Manning 219 AV

Winningest Coach: Tony Dungy 85-27-0

TEAMS OF THE NFL

JACKSONVILLE JAGUARS

The Jacksonville Jaguars were founded in 1993 and played the first season in 1995. The home field is TIAA Bank Field in Jacksonville, Florida. Which they have played their home games on for the past 23 years. They joined the NFL along with the Carolina Panthers for the 1995 season as league expansion teams.

They won the AFC Central (now defunct) championships in 1998 and then again in 1999. They became a member of the AFC South division in 2002. After a ten-season playoff drought, they qualified in 2017. Before 2007 they had managed to qualify for the playoffs seven times.

Wayne Weaver had was the first owner of the Jaguars up until the team was sold to Shahid Khan for around $770 million.

When the team was first formed by owner Wayne Weaver who was eventually given the NFL expansion franchise Tom Coughlin was appointed the teams first ever head coach. The Jaguars alongside the Panthers both broke records for the most wins by expansion teams. A record previously held by the Cincinnati Bengals set in 1968.

For the following four seasons, the Jaguars made it to the Playoffs with a team that consisted of players such as quarterback Mark Brunell, offensive lineman Tony Boselli, running back James Stewart and wide receiver Jimmy Smith.

From 2007 through to 2017 the Jaguars did not make another Playoff appearance. In 2017 the Jaguars beat the Houston Texans to clinch their first playoff game in ten years. They finished the season with a 10 – 6 giving them their first division win since 1999. Their defeat of the Buffalo Bills sent them to the Playoffs.

On the 14th January 2018, they defeated the Pittsburgh Steelers in Pittsburg with a 45 – 42 victory. This let the team advance to the AFC Championship Game for the third time in the team's history.

Their first AFC Championship game in eighteen years had them play against the New England Patriots. Although the Jaguars dominated most of the game, they lost by four points as they were defeated 24 – 20. The Jaguars defense earned the nickname "Sacksonville" as they proved to be a worthy opponent to the reigning champs.

The Jaguars have won three Division Championships and have appeared in seven Playoffs. They have yet to win a Conference or Super Bowl Championship. One of their main rivals is the Carolina Panthers who joined the NFL as an expansion team around the same time.

Currently, the Jaguars play at the TIAA Bank Field stadium for their home games. The stadium was initially the Jacksonville Municipal Stadium. In 2014, thanks to a substantial contribution from the team's owner, Shahid Khan, the stadium got a long overdue upgrade. These included the worlds largest video boards for the scoreboards. New cabana seating, pools and premium seating including 180 seats that are at field level.

Jacksonville Jaguars Franchise Encyclopedia

Seasons: 25 (1995 to 2019)

Record (W-L-T): 170-214-0

Playoff Record: 7-7

Super Bowls Won: 0 (0 Appearances)

Championships Won*: 0

All-time Passing Leader: Mark Brunell 2,184/3,616, 25,698 yds, 144 TD

All-time Rushing Leader: Fred Taylor 2,428 att, 11,271 yds, 62 TD

All-time Receiving Leader: Jimmy Smith 862 rec, 12,287 yds, 67 TD

All-time Scoring Leader: Josh Scobee 1,022 points

All-time AV Leader: Jimmy Smith 135 AV

Winningest Coach: Tom Coughlin 68-60-0

TEAMS OF THE NFL

TENNESSEE TITANS

Initially formed as the Houston Oilers in 1960 they were a charter member of the American Football League Eastern Division until 1969. With the NFL/AFL merge in 1970 they joined the NFL playing for the Central AFC division up until 1996. The Houston Oilers had one owner from their inception in 1960, Bud Adams and played their home field at the Jeppesen Stadium from 1960 through to 1964 where they moved to Rice Stadium for two years (1965 – 1967) before making the Houston Astrodome their home in 1968.

The Oilers won two AFL Championships (1960 and 1961), four AFL Division Championships (1960, 1961, 1962 and 1967) and appeared in five AFL playoffs (1960, 1961, 1962, 1967 and 1969). The merger with the NFL saw the team win two AFC Central Divisional titles (1991 and 1993) and appear in ten NFL Playoffs (1978, 1979, 1980, 1987, 1988, 1989, 1990, 1991, 1992 and 1993).

Bud Adams had been threatening to move the Oilers to Jacksonville, Florida since 1987 when his demands for greater improvements to both their current home stadium and then later fans hotel accommodations were not met. The team had also not fared well since the merger with the NFL and had battled to gain ground in order to rise up in the Leagues ranks.

After a 25-year battle to gain ground the Oilers won their first divisional NFL title in 1991 but narrowly missed winning their first Conference title game. In 1992 they made NFL history when they played the Buffalo Bills in a wild-card playoff game which became known as "The Comeback". The Oilers finished the season with a 10 – 6 regular season record.

They won another AFC title in 1993 when they had the best ever Texas season with a 12 – 4 regular season record. This season would be the last time the Oilers made the playoffs while they were still located in Texas. Their last season in Texas turned out to be quite a disastrous one for the teams as their imminent move to Tennessee had been announced resulting in the drop off of support for the Oilers.

They played their first two seasons as the "Tennessee Oilers" with their home stadium as the Liberty Bowl Memorial Stadium which is located in Memphis. They were still part of the AFC Central division. They were relocated once again to Nashville in 1998 and took up their home field as the Vanderbilt Stadium with their name being changed to the Tennessee Titans for the 1999 season.

Since becoming the Titans they have won one Conference Championship, one AFC Central Divisional Championship, and two AFC South (the division they are now part of) Championships. They have appeared in seven Playoff games and made it to the Super Bowl once. They played in the Super Bowl XXXIV and lost to the St. Louis Rams in 1999.

The team is still owned by KSA Industries that is now controlled by his daughters Amy Adams Strunk and Susie Adams Smith. Their current head coach is Mike Vrabel who recently joined as the team's head coach taking over from Mike Mularkey.

Houston Oilers/Tennessee Oilers/Tennessee Titans Franchise Encyclopedia

Seasons: 60 (1960 to 2019)

Record (W-L-T): 431-463-6

Playoff Record: 15-20

Super Bowls Won: 0 (1 Appearance)

Championships Won*: 2

All-time Passing Leader: Warren Moon 2,632/4,546, 33,685 yds, 196 TD

All-time Rushing Leader: Eddie George 2,733 att, 10,009 yds, 64 TD

All-time Receiving Leader: Ernest Givins 542 rec, 7,935 yds, 46 TD

All-time Scoring Leader: Al Del Greco 1,060 points

All-time AV Leader: Bruce Matthews 210 AV

Winningest Coach: Jeff Fisher 142-120-0

TEAMS OF THE NFL

DENVER BRONCOS

The Denver Broncos started in 1959 and played their first season in 1960 as a member club for the American Football League in the Western Division. They were established by Bob Howsam who was an American Sports Professional executive and who instrumental in the 1970 NFL/AFL merger.

Since their commencement, the team has changed ownership a few times the first being in 1961 when the team was purchased by Gerald Phipps, president of Gerald H. Phipps Construction. Phipps owned the team up until 1981 when it was bought by Edgar Kaiser Jr. before selling his majority shares in the team to Pat Bowlen in 1984. In 2014 Pat Bowlen relinquished control of the team to Joe Ellis the current team president due to a struggle with Alzheimer's but the team remains part of the Pat Bowlen Trust.

During their first ten years, the Bronco's were not that strong of a force and were barely competitive whilst playing in the AFL. With the 1970 NFL/AFL merge they were assigned to the AFC West division where they still currently play. It took the Bronco's another three years in the NFL before they had their first winning season in 1973 at 7-5-2 under the leadership of head coach John Ralston. Ralston joined the Bronco's in 1972 after which the team went on to have three winning seasons but had yet to make a playoff.

Ralston resigned during the 1977 season and in May that year, the Bronco's hired the former assistant coach of the New England Patriots, Red Miller. Who along with Craig Morton and the team's defense nicknamed the Orange Crush during this season the Bronco's made the Super Bowl (XII) for the first time in their teams' history! They were defeated by the 27 – 10 by the Dallas Cowboys but it was still a historic event for the Broncos.

The Broncos may have taken some time to get established but they have worked their way up to becoming one of the most successful NFL teams with only seven losing seasons behind them. From 1975 they have gone from strength to strength they have won three Super Bowl Championships (XXXII – 1977, XXXIII – 1978, 50 – 2015). They share the NFL Record for most Super Bowl loses (5) with the New England Patriots. The Broncos have won eight AFC Championships, fifteen AFC West Division Championships and appeared in twenty-two Playoff games.

Ten of the Bronco's players are in the Pro Football Hall of Fame and these players are Willie Brown, Gary Zimmerman, Ty Law, Champ Bailey, Floyd Little, John Elway, Shannon Sharpe, Terrel Davis, Tony Dorsett, and Brian Dawkins.

In 2012 the team signed former Indianapolis Colt's star quarterback Peyton Manning who played for the Bronco's up until his retirement in 2015. He led the Broncos to the Super Bowl 50 where they defeated the Carolina Panthers 24 – 10.

Their first home filed with the DU Stadium on the University of Denver, Colorado grounds for their first few home games before moving to the Mile High Stadium that same year. In 2001 the New Mile High Stadium was opened and named the Broncos Mile High Stadium which is the teams current home field.

Denver Broncos Franchise Encyclopedia

Seasons: 60 (1960 to 2019)

Record (W-L-T): 476-414-10

Playoff Record: 23-19

Super Bowls Won: 3 (8 Appearances)

Championships Won*: 3

All-time Passing Leader: John Elway 4,123/7,250, 51,475 yds, 300 TD

All-time Rushing Leader: Terrell Davis 1,655 att, 7,607 yds, 60 TD

All-time Receiving Leader: Rod Smith 849 rec, 11,389 yds, 68 TD

All-time Scoring Leader: Jason Elam 1,786 points

All-time AV Leader: John Elway 203 AV

Winningest Coach: Mike Shanahan 138-86-0

TEAMS OF THE NFL

KANSAS CITY CHIEFS

The Kansas City Chiefs started out as the Dallas Texans who were a charter member of the AFL playing for the Western Division and owned Lamar Hunt. The team was founded in 1960 and are not associated in any way to the NFL Dallas Texans that folded in 1952. Lamar Hunt is one of the founding members of the American Football League alongside Bud Adams. Both were denied football franchises by the NFL.

As the Dallas Texans, they won one AFL West Division Championship in 1962 along with the AFL Championship that same year. Their home field at the time was the Cotton Bowl in Dallas Texas and their head coach at the time was former Miami assistant coach Hank Stram.

The team took on their current name the Kansas City Chiefs in 1963 when they were relocated to Kansas City with their new home field the Municipal Stadium where they played until 1971. The team moved to the Arrowhead Stadium which was completely renovated in 2007 through to 2010.

Prior to the 1970 NFL merger, the Chiefs won two AFL Championships (1966 and 1969), appeared in three playoffs (1966, 1968 and 1969). They won the AFL – NFL Super Bowl Championship in 1969 (Super Bowl IV) which is the only Super Bowl they have ever won. They also became the second AFL team to beat an NFL team, the Minnesota Vikings at a World Championship Game. They also became the first AFL team to appear in more than one Super Bowl Championship.

Kansas City Chiefs Franchise Encyclopedia

Seasons: 60 (1960 to 2019)

Record (W-L-T): 469-419-12

Playoff Record: 10-19

Super Bowls Won: 1 (2 Appearances)

Championships Won*: 2

All-time Passing Leader: Len Dawson 2,115/3,696, 28,507 yds, 237 TD

All-time Rushing Leader: Jamaal Charles 1,332 att, 7,260 yds, 43 TD

All-time Receiving Leader: Tony Gonzalez 916 rec, 10,940 yds, 76 TD

All-time Scoring Leader: Nick Lowery 1,466 points

All-time AV Leader: Will Shields 157 AV

Winningest Coach: Hank Stram 124-76-10

In 1970 the Chiefs joined with the NFL as part of the merger with the AFL to play in the AFC West Division of the league. Since joining the NFL they have had nine AFC West Divisional titles and appeared in seventeen Playoffs the most recent being in 2018. The end of the 2018 season the team had lost twelve of their last eighteen playoff games which is one of the longest playoffs losing streaks in the history of the NFL.

There are twenty-three members of the Pro Football Hall of Fame that either spent the majority of their career with the Chiefs or at least some part of it. These players include Bobby Bell, Willie Lanier, Len Dawson, Buck Buchanan, Jan Stenerud, Mike Webster, Ty Law, and Johnny Robinson to name a few. They can also boast a few of their coaches and contributors that were enshrined who include Lamar Hunt, Marv Levy, Hank Stram, Bill Polian, and Bobby Beathard.

The Chiefs are one of sixteen organizations that have their own Hall of Fame to honor their former members, contributors and or players. Since the inception in 1970 of their Hall of Fame, they have inducted a new member each year. Behind the Green Bay Packers, the Chiefs have the second-most enshrines in their team Hall of Fame than any other franchises team Hall of Fame.

The team is still owned by the Hunt family and run by Chairman Clark Hunt along with General Manager Brett Veach and Head Coach Andy Reid.

TEAMS OF THE NFL

LOS ANGELES CHARGERS

The Los Angeles Chargers were founded in 1959 owned by Hilton Hotels Heir Barron Hilton. They started the first season as a member club of the AFL Western Division where they played until the NFL/AFL merger in 1970.

Pre the 1970 NFL merger the Chargers had won one AFL Championship game in 1963, five AFL Western Division Championships and appeared in five AFL Playoffs games. The team moved to San Diego where the name was changed to the San Diego Chargers in 1961 through the NFL/AFL merger.

Their initial home field for the first season in 1960 was the Los Angeles Memorial Coliseum before the team was moved to San Diego in 1961. Here they took up the home field at the Balboa Stadium in Balboa Park, San Diego. In 1967 they relocated to the newly constructed San Diego Stadium which was later renamed SDCCU Stadium. This became their home game base up until they were relocated back to Los Angeles in 2017.

After the NFL merger, the team was assigned to the AFC West Division where they won one AFC Conference Championships (1994), ten AFC West Division Championships and appeared in thirteen Playoffs games.

The Chargers were bought by Eugene Klein in 1966 before the majority of the shares were bought from him by Billionaire Real Estate developer Alex Spanos in 1984 after which he gradually bought up the rest of the co-owners shares in the team until he retained 97% of them. The last 3% was owned by restaurant owner George Pernicano. In 1993 the daily operations and running of the franchise had been taken over by Alex Spanos son Dean.

In 1994 the Chargers managed to make it to the Super Bowl (XXIX) for their first and only time in the team's history. They played against the San Francisco 49ers and were defeated 49 – 26. The team have yet to win an AFC Championship game but have made four appearances.

After a lot of negotiations an agreement was struck with the NFL for the Chargers to relocate back to Los Angeles this followed a year after the Rams return to the area. The team set up their home game filed at Dignity Health Sports Park where they currently play lead by head coach Anthony Lynn and General Manager Tom Telesco.

The team has seen twelve of its players inducted into the Pro Football Hall of Fame. These players include Lance Alworth, Ron Mix, Johnny Unitas, Deacon Jones, John Mackey, Dan Fouts, Larry Little, Kellen Winslow, Charlie Joiner, Fred Dean, Junior Seau and most recently LaDainian Tomlinson. Right up there with them is Sid Gillman who was the Chargers head coach from the team's beginnings in 1960 through to 1971.

Los Angeles/San Diego Chargers Franchise Encyclopedia

Seasons: 60 (1960 to 2019)

Record (W-L-T): 447-442-11

Playoff Record: 12-18

Super Bowls Won: 0 (1 Appearance)

Championships Won*: 1

All-time Passing Leader: Philip Rivers 4,518/7,000, 54,656 yds, 374 TD

All-time Rushing Leader: LaDainian Tomlinson 2,880 att, 12,490 yds, 138 TD

All-time Receiving Leader: Antonio Gates 955 rec, 11,841 yds, 116 TD

All-time Scoring Leader: John Carney 1,076 points

All-time AV Leader: Philip Rivers 191 AV

Winningest Coach: Sid Gillman 86-53-6

TEAMS OF THE NFL

OAKLAND RAIDERS

The Oakland Raiders were founded in 1960 and played their first professional regular season game as a member club for the American Football League Western Division. Their home field at the time was Kezar Stadium in San Francisco, California for their first season. In 1961 their home field became Candlestick Park for another season. From 1962 through to the 1965 season they played their home games at the Frank Youell Field in Oakland, California moving to the Oakland Coliseum from 1966 up until 1981.

Whilst still as a member of the AFL the Raiders won one AFL Championship (1967), three AFL West Division Championships and appeared in three AFL Playoffs. The 1970 NFL/AFL merge had them assigned to the AFC West Division. Between 1970 and 1982 they won two Super Bowl Championships (XI – 1976 and XV – 1980, two AFC Conference Championships (1976 and 1980), six AFC West Division Championships (1970, 1972, 1973, 1974, 1975 and 1976) and appeared in eight Playoff games.

In 1982 the Oakland Raiders franchise was moved to Los Angeles where they became known as the Los Angeles Raiders. They played under this name up until 1994 during which time the won one Super Bowl (XVIII – 1983), one AFC Conference Championship (1983), three AFC West Division Championships (1983, 1985 and 1990) and appeared in seven Playoffs.

The Raiders returned to Oakland and resumed the name of Oakland Raiders at the beginning of the 1995 season. Their home field was once again the Oakland Coliseum as it remains today. Since their return to Oakland and resuming their old name they have won one AFC Conference Championship (2002), three AFC West Division Championships and appeared in four Playoffs.

The team was purchased by Al Davis in 1972 with him remaining the majority shareholder until his death in 2011. His shares were passed onto Mark Davis, his son, who is still the team's majority shareholder. In 2017 with a 31 – 1 vote at the annual league member meeting it was determined that the Raiders would move to Las Vegas, Nevada in 2020 pending the completion of their new home stadium.

In 1962 Al Davis was hired as the head coach for the Raiders making him the youngest person in the history of professional football to hold this position at the age of 33. He became the AFL Commissioner in 1966 and the head coach position was offered to John Rauch two month before the NFL/AFL pending merger was announced. As his position as AFL Commissioner became obsolete with the merger Davis purchased a 10% interest in the team and returned as part owner thereof!

Al Davis was inducted into the Pro Football Hall of Fame with another fourteen players and ten contributors who spent the majority of or part of their pro football career with the Raiders. Players such as Jerry Rice, Tim Brown, Marcus Allen, Howie Long, and Ken Stabler to name a few inducted through the years.

Oakland/Los Angeles Raiders Franchise Encyclopedia

Seasons: 60 (1960 to 2019)

Record (W-L-T): 466-423-11

Playoff Record: 25-19

Super Bowls Won: 3 (5 Appearances)

Championships Won*: 3

All-time Passing Leader: Ken Stabler 1,486/2,481, 19,078 yds, 150 TD

All-time Rushing Leader: Marcus Allen 2,090 att, 8,545 yds, 79 TD

All-time Receiving Leader: Tim Brown 1,070 rec, 14,734 yds, 99 TD

All-time Scoring Leader: Sebastian Janikowski 1,799 points

All-time AV Leader: Jim Otto 154 AV

Winningest Coach: John Madden 103-32-7

TEAMS OF THE NFL

DALLAS COWBOYS

In 2015 the Cowboys were said to be the most valuable sports team in the world with a value of $4 billion U.S. In 2014 their generated revenue was $620 million U.S. Dollars a record in the history of U.S. sports team. They became the first NFL Franchise to be valued at $5 billion dollars in 2018 and made the Forbes most valued NFL team for the 12th year running.

The Cowboys were started after a much-heated rivalry had ignited between Washington Redskins owner George Marshall and soon to be the owner of the Dallas Cowboys Clint Murchinson Jr. After acquiring the rights to the Redskins team song Murchinson managed to strike up a deal with Marshall in order to get his vote for an NFL Expansion team franchise. The team had their first professional football season as a member club of the NFL Western Conference in 1960 to 1961. They were moved to the NFL Eastern Conference Capitol Division from 1967 through to 1969. With the NFL/AFL merger they were assigned to play in the NFC East Division where they still play.

Sports writers have contributed the Cowboys success to the patience and deep pockets of Murchinson. In 1984 he sold the Cowboys to Bum Bright who was the head of an investment syndicate. He, in turn, sold the team off in 1989 to Jerry Jones, a billionaire businessman who is still the owner, president, and general manager of the tea. His son, Stephen Jones is the current CEO of the Dallas Cowboys.

Out of the teams, eight Super Bowl Appearances they have won five NFL Championships played in eight NFC Championships plus two NFL Eastern Championships and an overall of twenty-four Division Championships. They have appeared in thirty-three Playoffs games and the only NFL team to have a record of twenty straight winning seasons from 1966 through to 1985. The team has only ever missed the Playoffs twice this was in 1974 and then again in 1984.

They have an extremely strong national following which is proven by the one-hundred and ninety consecutive sold-out games for both regular and postseason games since 2002. Their first home field was the Cotton Bowl on which they played from 1960 through to 1971 after which they moved to Texas Stadium for 1971 through to 2008 seasons. In 2009 they moved their home game field to the AT&T Stadium in Arlington, Texas. They still play at this stadium led by their head coach Jason Garrett.

The Cowboys have had twenty of their top players inducted into the Pro Football Hall of Fame. With coaches such as Tom Landry and Bill Parcells joining them along with a few other contributors including Jerry Jones.

Dallas Cowboys Franchise Encyclopedia

Seasons: 60 (1960 to 2019)

Record (W-L-T): 512-380-6

Playoff Record: 35-28

Super Bowls Won: 5 (8 Appearances)

Championships Won*: 5

All-time Passing Leader: Tony Romo 2,829/4,335, 34,183 yds, 248 TD

All-time Rushing Leader: Emmitt Smith 4,052 att, 17,162 yds, 153 TD

All-time Receiving Leader: Jason Witten 1,152 rec, 12,448 yds, 68 TD

All-time Scoring Leader: Emmitt Smith 986 points

All-time AV Leader: Emmitt Smith 163 AV

Winningest Coach: Tom Landry 250-162-6

TEAMS OF THE NFL

NEW YORK GIANTS

The New York Giants were founded in 1925 joining the NFL along with four other teams that same year. Tim Mara was the original founder of the team who is the only team of the five to still be in existence. They are also one of the oldest established NFL teams in the Northern United States. They started out playing at the Polo Grounds up until 1955 where they moved to Yankee Stadium for the 1956 season through to 1973. After that, they played at the Yale Bowl (1973 – 1974), Shea Stadium (1975), Giants Stadium (1976 – 2009) until they moved to their present home field at the MetLife Stadium in 2010.

Currently, they play in the NFC East Division which they have done since 1970. During their history, the Giants won four NFL Championship Games pre the 1970 merger with the AFL. Since the merger, they have won four Super Bowl Championships (XXI – 1986, XXV – 1990, XLII – 2007 and XLVI – 2011). They have won eleven Conference Championships, twenty-two NFL/NFC Division Championships and appeared in thirty-two Playoffs games since 1925.

They are number three in the NFL rankings with more Championship appearances than any other team in the league and they have featured twenty-eight hall of fame players. These players include the likes of Mel Hein, Y.A. Tittle, Lawrence Taylor, and Frank Gifford.

New York Giants Franchise Encyclopedia

Seasons: 95 (1925 to 2019)

Record (W-L-T): 692-596-33

Playoff Record: 24-25

Super Bowls Won: 4 (5 Appearances)

Championships Won*: 8

All-time Passing Leader: Eli Manning 4,804/7,972, 55,981 yds, 360 TD

All-time Rushing Leader: Tiki Barber 2,217 att, 10,449 yds, 55 TD

All-time Receiving Leader: Amani Toomer 668 rec, 9,497 yds, 54 TD

All-time Scoring Leader: Pete Gogolak 646 points

All-time AV Leader: Lawrence Taylor 182 AV

Winningest Coach: Steve Owen 153-100-17

As they share a common name with the New York Baseball team also the New York Giants. In 1937 the team's name was changed to New York Football Giants, Inc. which it is still called today even though the baseball team moved to San Francisco in 1957. Sports-Casters usually refer to the team as the New York Football Giants although they have other nicknames such as "Big Blue", "G-Men" and "Jints" or even "The Big Blue wrecking crew".

The Giant also has one of the oldest NFC East team rivalries going with the Philadelphia Eagles which dates back to 1933 and is fondly referred to as "the best NFL rivalry of the 21st century". From their very first game, the Giants were a success playing it as an away game in New Britain against All New Britain which they won 26 – 0 witnessed by a crowd of 10 000 people. They won their first season with a record 8 – 4.

They were awarded the NFL title in their third season after finishing with a league record of 11-1-1. Their fourth season was not such a success and in order to ensure his team success the following season, Mara went after quarterback Benny Friedman of the Detroit Wolverines. In order to acquire him, Mara had to buy the entire squad and merge the two teams keeping the Giants name.

The team is currently owned by Tim Mara's grandson John Mara and Steve Tisch. Dave Gettleman is the teams General Manager and the Pat Shurmur as their head coach.

ELI MANNING

TEAMS OF THE NFL

PHILADELPHIA EAGLES

The Philadelphia Eagles were established in 1933 by a syndicate led by Bert Bell. They acquired the rights to a Philadelphia NFL Franchise after the Frankford Yellow Jackets folded in 1931. They have played in three different NFL divisions since their start from the NFL Eastern Division in 1933 to 1949, American Conference 1950 to 1952 and the Eastern Conference Capitol Division from 1967 to 1969.

Between 1933 and 1969 they won three NFL Championships, one Conference Championship in 1960 and three NFL East Division Championships (1947, 1948 and 1949). During this period they appeared in four Playoffs games.

During World War II due to loss of players the Eagles and Pittsburgh Steelers were forced to merge for the 1943 season. They were officially registered as "Phil-Pitt Combine" but they were unofficially called "Steagles" which is how the team was fondly remembered during this trying time. After finishing the season with a 5-4-1 record the merger was dissolved when the season finished.

The Eagles had one of the best seasons ever as a single team again in 1944 under head coach Greasy Neale and their star running back Steve Van Buren. Although they did not go on to reach a title game until 1947, they were a force to be reckoned with. Their loss to the Chicago Cardinals did not deter them the following year as the stormed through to another Title game winning their first NFL Championship defeating the Cardinals in a 7-0 victory.

They went on to win the title game again in 1949 which they won once again with a 14 – 0 victory over the Los Angeles Rams. The game was one that was remembered for the torrent of rain that washed over the game and made the field into a mud pit. It was also the first NFL Title game to be played in the Western United States.

The team was purchased by current owner Jeffery Lurie in 1994 from Norman Braman for $195 million U.S. dollars. The team now ranks as the 10th most valuable team in the NFL with its current value estimated at $2.65 billion U.S. dollars.

Since the 1970 merger with the AFL, the Eagles were assigned to the NFC East Division where they currently play. They have since won their first NFL Super Bowl Title (LII – 2017), three Conference Championships, ten Division Championships and have appeared in twenty-two Playoffs games.

Throughout their history they have played on six different home fields starting with Baker Bowl from 1933 to 1935, Philadelphia Municipal Stadium from 1936 to 1939 and again in 1941, Connie Mack Stadium in 1940 then again from 1940 through to 1957. From 1958 through to 1970 their home game field was Franklin Field, followed by Veterans Stadium from 1971 through to 2002. In 2003 they moved their home game field to Lincoln Financial Field where they still play led by head coach Doug Pederson.

Philadelphia Eagles F Franchise Encyclopedia

Seasons: 87 (1933 to 2019)

Record (W-L-T): 577-601-26

Playoff Record: 23-22

Super Bowls Won: 1 (3 Appearances)

Championships Won*: 4

All-time Passing Leader: Donovan McNabb 2,801/4,746, 32,873 yds, 216 TD

All-time Rushing Leader: LeSean McCoy 1,461 att, 6,792 yds, 44 TD

All-time Receiving Leader: Harold Carmichael 589 rec, 8,978 yds, 79 TD

All-time Scoring Leader: David Akers 1,323 points

All-time AV Leader: Reggie White 126 AV

Winningest Coach: Andy Reid 130-93-1

TEAMS OF THE NFL

WASHINGTON REDSKINS

In 1932 the Boston Braves were formed in Boston, Massachusetts by team owner George Preston Marshall. Their home field was the Braves Field which was also the home field for the Boston Braves Baseball team. The team was a member club of the National Football League playing for the Eastern Division.

In 1933 the team was moved to Fenway Park as their home ground with a result the owners changed the team's name to the Boston Redskins. Marshall then hired William Dietz who was part Sioux as the team's head coach. In their final season as the Boston Redskins, the team won the NFL Eastern Division Championship in 1936 and appeared in the Playoffs.

After five years in Boston, New England the Redskins were relocated to Washington D.C. in 1937. Here they shared the Giffith Stadium with the Washington Senators baseball team. They won their first division title in their first season as the Washington Redskins going on to win their first NFL Championship game.

Pre the 1970 NFL/AFL merger the Washington Redskins won two NFL Championship games (1937 and again in 1942), five NFL Eastern Division Championships and made five Playoffs games.

Today the team is considered by Forbes to be the fourth most valuable NFL team and the tenth most valuable sports team in the world. With a net worth of an estimated $3.1 billion U.S. dollars. They have a single-season attendance record that is in the NFL's top ten.

In 1961 a 25% interest in the team was bought by Jack Cook who was a sports broadcaster who had moved to America from Canada. In 1974 the majority shareholder and team founder George Marshall suffered a stroke and Cooke bought his shares to become the majority shareholder of the team. By 1985 he became the sole owner of the team and along with his head coach Joe Gibbs, the Redskins went on to three Super Bowls (XVII 1982, XXII 1987, XXVI 1991).

In 1997 the team moved their home game field from RFK Stadium to the FedExField where they currently play. The field was originally called the Jack Kent Cooke Stadium which was bought along with the team in by Daniel Snyder in 1999. Since then the team has yet to have a decent season and have had eight different head coaches in 17 seasons.

After being the 6th most popular NFL team in 2003 the team's popularity has dropped to number ten. Snyder has been highly criticized since taking over the Redskins and has not made himself very popular with the public especially when he sued ticket holders that were unable to pay for their season tickets during the U.S. recession of 2008-2009. There has been a lot of fan discontent with rising ticket prices, unfavorable stadium conditions and the growing controversy over the Redskins name being deemed offensive to Native Americans.

The Redskins have not made a playoff or Division Championship since 2015 or won a conference game since 1991. The team is currently managed by Dan Snyder, his president Bruce Allen and head coach Jay Gruden.

Washington Redskins Franchise Encyclopedia

Seasons: 88 (1932 to 2019)

Record (W-L-T): 600-590-28

Playoff Record: 23-19

Super Bowls Won: 3 (5 Appearances)

Championships Won*: 5

All-time Passing Leader:
Joe Theismann 2,044/3,602, 25,206 yds, 160 TD

All-time Rushing Leader:
John Riggins 1,988 att, 7,472 yds, 79 TD

All-time Receiving Leader:
Art Monk 888 rec, 12,026 yds, 65 TD

All-time Scoring Leader:
Mark Moseley 1,206 points

All-time AV Leader:
Darrell Green 148 AV

Winningest Coach:
Joe Gibbs 154-94-0

TEAMS OF THE NFL

CHICAGO BEARS

The Chicago Bears were established in 1920 as the Decatur Stanleys in Decatur, Illinois. They were moved to Chicago in 1921 and the team's name was changed to Chicago Stanley. Along with the Arizona Cardinals (who also had their start in Chicago) they are the only other remaining franchises left of the NFL founding member teams. The started out playing at Stately Field in 1920 moving to Wrigley Field after relocating in 1921 where they stayed through the 1970 season. Their name was changed to the Chicago Bears in 1922 and is the number under which they still play as to date.

The team was originally founded by A.E. Staley Company but was sold to George Halas and Dutch Sternaman in 1921. By 1932 George Halas was the majority shareholder of the team which he kept until 1983 when it was passed to his daughter Virginia Halas McCaskey. Currently, the team is managed by Ryan Pace with head coach Matt Nagy.

In the early years the team played for the NFL Western Division (1933 – 1949), the National conference (1950 – 1952) and then the Western Conference Central Division (1967 – 1969) pre-NFL/AFL merge of 1970.

After the merge, the team was assigned to the NFC Central Division where it played from the 1970 season through to the 2001 season. In 2002 it was assigned to the NFC North Division where they currently play.

Currently, the teams home games are played at Soldier Field where they played from 1971 through to 2001, they relocated to Memorial Stadium in 2002 when the stadiums interior was gutted and remodeled ready for the Bears to move back in 2003. They currently play at Soldier Field which is the second-oldest field in the NFL. Due to the 2002 renovations, the building was delisted as a historical landmark it is also the third smallest stadium in the NFL.

Before 1970 merge the Bears had appeared in eleven Playoffs games, won ten NFL Western Division Titles, two NFL Western Conference Titles and eight NFL Championship titles. After the merge, they appeared in fifteen Playoffs games, eleven NFC Central/North Division Championships and two NFC Conference Championships. The won their first and currently only Super Bowl (XX) game in 1985.

The Bears hold the NFL record for the most enshrined members in the Pro Football Hall of fame of which there have been 28. Their first inductees were in 1963 and were their founder/owner George Halas, "The Galloping Ghost" halfback Harrold Edward "Red" Grange and another halfback Bronko Nagurski. Between 1963 and 1967 another 14 members of the Bears Franchise were inducted. With their most recent of inductees being in 2018 Brian Urlacher who was a Middle linebacker for the Bears who spent his entire pro football career of thirteen years with the team.

They also have the highest amount of retired jersey numbers than any other team in the NFL. The last of the fourteen retired numbers was the number 89 jersey worn by former Bears tight and Head Coach, Mike Ditka.

Chicago Bears Franchise Encyclopedia

Seasons: 100 (1920 to 2019)

Record (W-L-T): 761-583-42

Playoff Record: 17-19

Super Bowls Won: 1 (2 Appearances)

Championships Won*: 9

All-time Passing Leader: Jay Cutler 2,020/3,271, 23,443 yds, 154 TD

All-time Rushing Leader: Walter Payton 3,838 att, 16,726 yds, 110 TD

All-time Receiving Leader: Johnny Morris 356 rec, 5,059 yds, 31 TD

All-time Scoring Leader: Robbie Gould 1,207 points

All-time AV Leader: Walter Payton 168 AV

Winningest Coach: George Halas 318-148-31

WALTER PAYTON

TEAMS OF THE NFL

DETROIT LIONS

The Detroit Lions was founded as the Portsmouth Spartans in 1929, they were originally owned by the city of Portsmouth, Ohio. The team took in members from other defunct semi-pro of pro football teams. They joined the NFL as the Portsmouth Spartans in 1930 led by head coach Hal Griffen playing at the Universal Stadium as their home field. The finished eighth in the league in 1930 ending the season with a score of 5-6-3. At the time there were only eleven member teams of the NFL.

The Spartans had an outstanding season in 1932 where the game against the Green Bay Packers became known as the "iron man game". The Spartans head coach at the time, Potsy Clark, had the entire game played with only eleven players refusing any substitutions during the match. They won with a 19-0 victory over the Packers. The also ended the season tied with the Chicago Bears for first place.

In 1934 the Spartans were sold to Detroit radio station, WJR, owner George Richards who moved the team to Detroit. They played the 1934 season as the Detroit Lions in order to complement Detroit's Major Basketball League Team the Detroit Tigers. The Lions new home game field became the University of Detroit Stadium from 1934 through to 1940, Tiger Stadium from 1938 – 1939 and again in 1941 through to 1974). In 1975 they were moved to the Pontiac Silverdome where they played through to the 2001 season before relocating to their current home game field Ford Field in 2002.

Detroit Lions Franchise Encyclopedia

Seasons: 90 (1930 to 2019)

Record (W-L-T): 559-658-32

Playoff Record: 7-13

Super Bowls Won: 0 (0 Appearances)

Championships Won*: 4

All-time Passing Leader: Matthew Stafford 3,372/5,405, 38,526 yds, 237 TD

All-time Rushing Leader: Barry Sanders 3,062 att, 15,269 yds, 99 TD

All-time Receiving Leader: Calvin Johnson 731 rec, 11,619 yds, 83 TD

All-time Scoring Leader: Jason Hanson 2,150 points

All-time AV Leader: Barry Sanders 150 AV

Winningest Coach: Wayne Fontes 66-67-0

In 1940 Fred Mandel bought the Lions franchise which he owned up until 1948 when it was purchased by a group of Detroit businessmen. In 1965 the franchise was once again sold to William Clay Ford and it is still owned by them. Currently being managed by Bob Quinn and coached by head coach Matt Patricia.

Since 1934 the Lions have won four NFL Championships (pre 1970 AFL-NFL merge), four NFL Conference Championships (1952, 1953.1954 and 1957), five NFL Division Championships, three NFC Central Division Championships and appeared in seventeen Playoffs games. They have yet to win a Super Bowl Championship making one of the four NFL teams that have not yet won this title. They are, however, the only NFL franchise that has functional during all fifty-two Super Bowls without ever having appeared in one.

They currently have six retired jersey numbers with the latest being that of Chuck Huges, number 85 who played for the Lions from 1970 to 1971. The jersey was retired in his honor after he died of a heart attack during a game in 1971. Although Kevin Johnson acquired permission to wear the jersey from the Huges family for the 2005 season that he played with the Lions. He had worn the number 85 most of his football career as a wide receiver.

The Lions have had twenty franchise members inducted into the Pro Football Hall of Fame with the most recent being Dick Stanfel in 2016, Dick LeBeau in 2010 and Charlie Sanders in 2007.

TEAMS OF THE NFL

GREEN BAY PACKERS

Based in Green Bay, Wisconsin the Green Bay Packers are the third oldest team in the NFL league, the only non-profit major league professional sports team that is community owned. They are also the only team that the NFL will allow to be fan operated and they are located in the smallest NFL media market. They are truly a unique team and to top off their uniqueness the team are the NFL's oldest franchise to have operated in the same location since their inception. The Packers are the last of the "small town" teams to play in the NFL and they have played Lambeau Field since 1957.

They were established as the Green Bay Acme Packers in 1919 and played as an independent team against other semi-pro clubs located in the Midwest and Wisconsin areas until the end of the 1920 season. Now called the Green Bay Packers they joined the NFL in 1921 and played for the Western division, National Division and Western Conference Central division before the NFL/AFL merger. In 1970 up until 2001 the played for the NFC Central Division and were switched to the NFC Northern Division in 2002 where they still currently play.

They can trace their roots back to a Green Bay team that has played in the city since 1896 with the team that was established in 1919 was founded by Earl Lambeau (known as Curly) and George Whitney Calhoun. Although they are the smallest major league professional sports market in the USA, Forbes has ranked the Green Bay Packers as the 26th most valuable sports franchise in the world and worth $2.35 billion American Dollars.

The publicly held corporation that owns the franchise is called Green Bay Packers, Inc. which is governed by a Board of Directors. The Chairman and CEO of the company currently are Mark H. Murphy, the General Manager is Brian Gutekunst and the Head Coach is Matt LaFleur. The team has played on a few home fields until it landed at Lambeau Field in 1957 having originally started playing at Hagemeister Park from 1919 through to 1922 after which their home field changed another six times between 1923 through to 1953 but they were always located in their home town.

The Packers have produced twenty-four Pro Football Hall of Fame players, with one coach, Victor Lombardi inducted in 1971 and General Manager Ron Wolf inducted in 2015. They may be a small-town team, but they have made a huge impact on the NFL having won thirteen League Championships. These include eleven NFL Championships, two AFL-NFL Championships and two Super Bowl Championships (XXXI – 1996 and XLV – 2010). The Packers have won nine Conference championships, eighteen Division championships and appeared in the Playoffs thirty-two times.

A long-standing rivalry is held between the Minnesota Vikings, Chicago Bears and Detroit Lions all of which were members of the NFC North division of the NFL. The Packers have played against each of these over 100 times through the Leagues history and against them, all the Packers hold the highest winning record. Their rivalry with the Chicago Bears goes back to 1921 when they first joined the league making one of the oldest rivalries in the NFL.

Green Bay Packers Franchise Encyclopedia

Seasons: 99 (1921 to 2019)

Record (W-L-T): 743-571-38

Playoff Record: 34-22

Super Bowls Won: 4 (5 Appearances)

Championships Won*: 13

All-time Passing Leader:
Brett Favre 5,377/8,754, 61,655 yds, 442 TD

All-time Rushing Leader:
Ahman Green 1,851 att, 8,322 yds, 54 TD

All-time Receiving Leader:
Donald Driver 743 rec, 10,137 yds, 61 TD

All-time Scoring Leader:
Mason Crosby 1,469 points

All-time AV Leader:
Brett Favre 222 AV

Winningest Coach:
Curly Lambeau 209-104-21

BRETT FAVRE

TEAMS OF THE NFL

MINNESOTA VIKINGS

The Vikings are an expansion team that joined the NFL in 1960 when they were established by a group of owners namely Max Winter, E. William Boyer, H.P. Skoglund, Ole Haugsrud and Bernard H. Ridder Jr. In 1960 Bert Rose was appointed as the first General Manager of the team and Norm Van Brocklin was selected to be the Head Coach.

Originally, they played for the NFL Western Conference Central Division with their home field being the Metropolitan Stadium where they played from 1961 through to the end of the 1981 season. Their first ever game was played on the 5th August 1961 against the Dallas Cowboys in a pre-season game and was defeated 38 – 13. However, their first ever NFL regular-season game saw the Vikings beat the Chicago Bears 37 – 13.

The early years of the team saw them improve up until 1969 when they won the NFL Championship which was the final one before the AFL-NFL merger. Through their League years, the Vikings have won four Conference Championships, twenty Division Championships and appeared in the Playoff twenty-nine times. They have had nineteen players inducted into the Pro Football Hall of Fame along with Head Coach Bud Grant and General Manager Jim Finks. The Vikings have six retired jersey numbers which are number 10 - last worn by Fran Tarkenton, 53 - last worn by Mick Tingelhoff, 70 – last worn by Jim Marshall, 77 – last worn by the late Korey Stringer, 80 – last worn by Cris Carter and 88 last worn by Alan Page.

Minnesota Vikings Franchise Encyclopedia

Seasons: 59 (1961 to 2019)

Record (W-L-T): 478-397-11

Playoff Record: 20-29

Super Bowls Won: 0 (4 Appearances)

Championships Won*: 0

All-time Passing Leader: Fran Tarkenton 2,635/4,569, 33,098 yds, 239 TD

All-time Rushing Leader: Adrian Peterson 2,418 att, 11,747 yds, 97 TD

All-time Receiving Leader: Cris Carter 1,004 rec, 12,383 yds, 110 TD

All-time Scoring Leader: Fred Cox 1,365 points

All-time AV Leader: Carl Eller 165 AV

Winningest Coach: Bud Grant 158-96-5

Minnesota Vikings Ring of Honor is where the team lists its own alumni player bios and legends who have played for or contributed to making the team great. The franchise is currently owned by Zygi Wilf who also acts as Chairman along with Mark Wilf as President, Rick Spielman as General Manager and Head Coach is Mike Zimmer. The currently play their home games the U.S. Bank Stadium where they have been since 2016.

They may only have won one NFL Championship in the history, but they hold one of the Leagues highest winning percentages, are one of six teams to win fifteen games in a regular season, they have also won an average of three games in every season. Although they did not win the title the Vikings have played in four Super Bowls – IV, VIII, IX and XI.

The Minnesota Vikings were named as such as Minnesota is the centre of Scandinavian American Culture. Their fans embrace their teams' culture by wearing Helga Hats that are hand assembled in the Twin Cities area. The hats are purple in colour with white horns and blonde braids meant to mimic the helmets once worn by Viking warriors. The team's mascot is Victor the Viking and their fight song is Skol, Vikings! At their home games, their fans kitted out in their helmets, cheer for their team and play their Gjallarhorn (Viking Horn) to announce their joy after the Vikings have made a major play, their first touchdown. The horn is also often played during pre-game ceremonies along with the flash cannon that fires if the Vikings make a touchdown.

TEAMS OF THE NFL

ATLANTA FALCONS

The Atlanta Falcons were established in 1965 by Rankin Smith who was offered an NFL expansion franchise in order to stop him joining their rival league the AFL. Their first official season was in 1966 with their home field being Atlanta-Fulton Country Stadium on which they played from 1966 through to the end of their 1991 season. Currently, the team plays for the NFC South Division and their home field is currently the Mercedes-Benz Stadium which they moved to in 2017.

The Falcons are currently owned by majority shareholder Arthur Blank, CEO is Rich McKay, General Manager is Thomas Dimitroff and the Head Coach is Dan Quinn. Since the team began they have as yet to win a League Championship, they have won two Conference Championships, six Division Championships and made fourteen Playoff appearances. They have played in two Super Bowls the first being against the Denver Broncos who defeated them 34 – 19 in 1998 (Super Bowl XXXIII). Their second Super Bowl appearance was in 2017 at the Super Bowl LI where they played against the New England Patriots and lost 34 – 28.

Between 1962 and 1964 the AFL staged a few exhibitions Pro Football matches in Atlanta the first in 1962 and the second in 1964. The Atlanta Stadium was built in 1965 in order to attract Major League Baseball to the city. As the AFL tried to close in on Atlanta and secure the rights to the stadium Pete Rozelle, who at the time was the NFL Commissioner forced the cities hand to choose between the two leagues. By the end of June 1965, the city of Atlanta decided to back Rankin Smith and the NFL who awarded him the Atlanta expansion franchise.

Two new expansion teams were being planned for by the NFL, but they were not supposed to be added until 1967. But in order for the league to claim Atlanta before the AFL did force their hand to assign a new franchise team two years earlier than planned. For the next two years, the League had to play with an odd number of teams (15 in total) which meant that one team per week did not get to play a game so each team could play fourteen games over fifteen weeks. The next new expansion team joined the league in 1967 as the sixteenth team and that was the New Orleans Saints.

The Atlanta Falcons franchise was bought for $8.5 million which at the time was the highest amount ever paid for a team in NFL history. The team was named the Falcons was suggested by a school teacher Miss Julia Elliot. In her suggestion, she wrote "the Falcon is proud and dignified, with great courage and fight. It never drops its prey. It is deadly and a great sporting tradition". Their Mascot became Freddie Falcon and the team colours currently are red, black, silver and white.

The team has had fourteen players inducted into the Pro Football Hall of Fame alongside Head Coach Norm Van Brocklin.

Their biggest rivals are the New Orleans Saints with which the Falcons leads the series with 52 – 48. The other rival is the Carolina Panthers with the Falcons once again leading the series 27 – 17.

Atlanta Falcons Franchise Encyclopedia

Seasons: 54 (1966 to 2019)

Record (W-L-T): 358-452-6

Playoff Record: 10-14

Super Bowls Won: 0 (2 Appearances)

Championships Won*: 0

All-time Passing Leader: Matt Ryan 4,052/6,201, 46,720 yds, 295 TD

All-time Rushing Leader: Gerald Riggs 1,587 att, 6,631 yds, 48 TD

All-time Receiving Leader: Roddy White 808 rec, 10,863 yds, 63 TD

All-time Scoring Leader: Matt Bryant 1,122 points

All-time AV Leader: Matt Ryan 166 AV

Winningest Coach: Mike Smith 66-46-0

TEAMS OF THE NFL

CAROLINA PANTHERS

The Carolina Panthers were established in 1993 by Jerry Richardson who was a former Baltimore Colts Flanker/Halfback from 1959 through to 1960. Richardson owned the Panthers for twenty-five years before selling the team to David Tepper in May 2018. Tepper's top personnel included Tom Glick as President and Marty Hurney as the team's General Manager.

The Panthers played their first official season in 1995 for the NFL as a member club of the NFC West Division up until they were switched to the NFC South for the 2002 season where they currently play. During their first season in 1995, they played their home field at Memorial Stadium in Clemson, South Carolina before moving their current stadium in Charlotte in 1996. The Bank of America Stadium as it is known today opened in 1996 as Ericsson Stadium. In 2004 The Bank of America bought the naming rights to the stadium. The stadium is legally registered as Panthers Stadium, LLC and is one of the few home stadiums owned by an NFL team.

Head Coach Ron Rivera has been with the Panthers since 2011 and has led the Panthers to four Playoffs. During their history, the team have reached the Super Bowl twice although they did not win either of the League Championship games. They played the New England Patriots for the Super Bowl XXXVIII titled in 2003 but lost 29 – 32. On the 7 February 2016, the Panthers played the Bronco's for the Super Bowl 50 but defeated 10 – 24. They have won two Conference Championships, six Division Titles and appeared in eight Playoffs in their twenty-five years in the League.

The Panthers were the twenty-ninth member team of the NFL and started as an expansion franchise the same year as the Jacksonville Jaguars. As NFC West needed to increase its team size to five the Panthers were assigned to it. The New Orleans Saints and Atlanta Falcons, two other south-eastern teams already competed in this division. Dom Capers, who was the defensive coordinator for the Pittsburgh Steelers became the Panthers first head coach.

In their first season in the League, the Panthers finished the season 7 – 9 making NFL history as the best performance from a first-year expansion team ever. Their second season saw them do even better than their first when they went on to beat the Dallas Cowboys, who were the current Super Bowl defending champions at the time, in the divisional round. They were, however, beaten in the NFC Championship round by the Green Bay Packers, who went on to win the Super Bowl that year, The following two years were not the best for the team when they slipped to a 7-9 finish in 1997 and 4 – 12 in 1998 which culminated in Dom Capers being replaced.

Carolina Panthers Franchise Encyclopedia

Seasons: 25 (1995 to 2019)

Record (W-L-T): 190-193-1

Playoff Record: 9-8

Super Bowls Won: 0 (2 Appearances)

Championships Won*: 0

All-time Passing Leader: Cam Newton 2,321/3,891, 28,469 yds, 182 TD

All-time Rushing Leader: Jonathan Stewart 1,699 att, 7,318 yds, 51 TD

All-time Receiving Leader: Steve Smith 836 rec, 12,197 yds, 67 TD

All-time Scoring Leader: John Kasay 1,482 points

All-time AV Leader: Cam Newton 122 AV

Winningest Coach: John Fox 73-71-0

CAM NEWTON

TEAMS OF THE NFL

NEW ORLEANS SAINTS

The New Orleans Saints were founded in 1966 by the City of New Orleans, David Dixon and John W. Mecom in 1966. They played their first official season in 1967 as a member of the NFL Eastern Conference with their home game field the Tulane Stadium. As New Orleans has a large Catholic foundation the fans often sing "When the Saints Go Marching In" at home games. They have two official mascots Gumbo the Dog and Sir Saint their second one.

For their first twenty years as a team, they only managed to achieve .500 twice until 1987 when they had the first winning season and qualified for the Playoffs. They lost 44 – 10 to the Minnesota Vikings but it was enough to spur the team and end the 1988 season with a 10-6 record even though they did not reach the Playoffs.

They got their first ever Playoffs win in 2000 when they defeated the reigning Super Bowl Champs at the time the St. Louis Rams 31 – 28. The Saints have won one Super Bowl (XLIV – 2009) Championship in which they defeated the Indianapolis Colts 31 – 17. It is the only Super Bowl they have appeared in. They have won one Conference Championship, seven Division Championships and appeared in twelve Playoffs.

In 1970 Gayle Benson, widow of Tom Benson and owner of the Saints inherited the team upon her husband's death. Originally the team was supposed to have been bequeathed to his child and grandchildren. The will was widely disputed when the family tried to get Tom declared mentally unfit before his death and Gayle labelled a gold digger due to her past exploits and arrests with her previous husband. But he was declared mentally fit and allowed to change his will.

A former personal assistant of Tom Benson filed a lawsuit against the New Orleans Saints and Gayle Benson for racism and federal labour law violations. He was awarded compensation for the labour law violations but ruled against in terms of racism. The team is currently owned by the 72-year-old Gayle Benson who was heard to say that she would own the Saints for the rest of her life. The teams current President is Dennis Lauscha, General Manager is Mickey Loomis and Head Coach is Sean Payton. Their current home game field is the Mercedes Benz Superdome which was damaged in 2005 by Hurricane Katrina and the team were forced to play their home games at a few different stadiums such as Tiger Stadium, Alamodome and Giant Stadium until the Mercedes-Benz Superdome was reopened in 2006.

During Hurricane Katrina, the Superdome provided temporary shelter for those who were displaced by the devastation the hurricane left behind. It was damaged with parts of its roof torn off and flooding. It was fully refurbished after the hurricane and reopened for the Saints 2006 season. In 2011 Mercedes-Benz bought the naming rights to the stadium and its name was officially changed on the 23 October 2011.

New Orleans Saints Franchise Encyclopedia

Seasons: 53 (1967 to 2019)

Record (W-L-T): 362-435-5

Playoff Record: 9-11

Super Bowls Won: 1 (1 Appearance)

Championships Won*: 1

All-time Passing Leader: Drew Brees 5,461/7,974, 62,089 yds, 440 TD

All-time Rushing Leader: Deuce McAllister 1,429 att, 6,096 yds, 49 TD

All-time Receiving Leader: Marques Colston 711 rec, 9,759 yds, 72 TD

All-time Scoring Leader: Morten Andersen 1,318 points

All-time AV Leader: Drew Brees 207 AV

Winningest Coach: Sean Payton 118-74-0

TEAMS OF THE NFL
TAMPA BAY BUCCANEERS

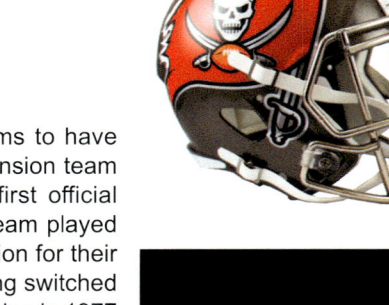

One of the newer teams to have joined as an NFL expansion team in 1974 playing their first official season in 1976. The team played for the AFC West Division for their first season before being switched to the NFC Central division in 1977 through to 2001 where they started playing in the NFC South division for the 2002 season where they still play.

Their current home game field is Raymond James Stadium which they have played at since 1998. Prior to that, they played at the Tampa Stadium. The team was originally founded by owner Hugh Culverhouse who appointed John McKay as the Head Coach. The team gained fame as the only team to lose an entire 14-game season which included five games in which they did not score.

In 1995 Malcolm Glazer bought the Buccaneers from the estate of the late Hugh Culverhouse paying $192 million which was an NFL record at the time of the purchase. Since then the team started the thrive under the new ownership winning one-hundred and thirty-one regular season games, made it to seven Playoffs and made it to their first Super Bowl XXXVII in 2002. The Buccanneers won 21 – 48 over the Oakland Raiders to take home the NFL League Title.

Nicknamed "The Bucs" they have won one Conference Championship, six Division Championships and had ten Playoff appearances. The end of the 2018 season saw the Buccanneers gather an overall record of 266-424-1, having played forty-three seasons.

Tampa Bay Buccaneers Franchise Encyclopedia

Seasons: 44 (1976 to 2019)

Record (W-L-T): 260-415-1

Playoff Record: 6-9

Super Bowls Won: 1 (1 Appearance)

Championships Won*: 1

All-time Passing Leader: Vinny Testaverde 1,126/2,160, 14,820 yds, 77 TD

All-time Rushing Leader: James Wilder 1,575 att, 5,957 yds, 37 TD

All-time Receiving Leader: Mike Evans 395 rec, 6,103 yds, 40 TD

All-time Scoring Leader: Martin Gramatica 592 points

All-time AV Leader: Derrick Brooks 191 AV

Winningest Coach: Jon Gruden 57-55-0

The team is still owned by the Glazer family with Bryan, Joel and Edward Glazier Chairmen, Jason Licht the General Manager and Bruce Arians the Head Coach. The team has had six players inducted into the Pro Football Hall of Fame alongside GM/VP Ron Wold and Coach Tony Dungy. They have retired only three numbers which are 55 – last worn by Derrick Brooks, 63 – last worn by Lee Roy Selmon and 99 – last worn by Warren Sapp.

The Tampa Bay franchise was not originally awarded to Hugh Culverhouse, who was a wealth tax attorney. Tom McCloskey was awarded it but got into a financial dispute with the NFL who then sought alternative owners for the franchise. Having filed antitrust lawsuits against the NFL in which he accused them of blocking his purchase of the Baltimore Colts the NFL agreed to give Culverhouse priority for the next NFL franchise team as part of his settlement.

The team name Buccaneers arose from a name the team contest inspired by a mythical Florida Pirate José Gaspar. The name was initially opposed as businessmen from St. Petersburg felt that it emphasized Tampa and excluded other Bay Area cities. Pete Rozelle encouraged their support of the name and the "Bucco Bruce" winking pirate logo. The logo was designed by Lamar Sparkman who was an artist for the Tampa Tribune.

The Buccanneers current mascot is Captain Fear, the team wears what they call their Gold Rush colours consisting of Buccaneer red, pewter and Bay orange. Their logo is a skull within a flag.

TEAMS OF THE NFL
ARIZONA CARDINALS

The Arizona Cardinals are the oldest established football team in the NFL as well as one of the only two teams left that were part of the inaugural NFL roster. They were founded in 1898 by which is over one-hundred and twenty years ago. Their first official season playing for the NFL was in 1920 when their home field was Normal Park, Chicago and they were known as Chicago Cardinals. For 1944 season their name was changed to Card-Pitt with a forced temporary merger between the Cardinal and the Pittsburgh Steelers. This was the second merge for the Steelers who had merged with the Eagles in 1943 to form the Steagles. They resumed playing as the Chicago Cardinals when the merger was dissolved for the 1945 season through to the 1959 season.

Chris O'Brien was the first owner of the Cardinals in 1920 up until 1929 when it was taken over by Dr David Jones from 1929 through to 1932 when he sold it to Charles Bidwell who did not announce ownership until he sold his stock in the Chicago Bears in 1933. Upon Charles Bidwell's death in 1947 the team's ownership went to his daughter Violet Bidwell Wolfner who after the teams losing year and almost reach a state of bankruptcy became interested in the idea of relocating the team in the late 1950s.

The team was moved to St Louis and played as the St. Louis Cardinals from the 1960 season through to the end of the 1987 season. They stayed in St. Louis for twenty-eight years. Upon Violet's death, the team was left to her sons Charles Bidwill, Jr. and Bill Bidwill who become the club's president and vice president. In 1972 Bill purchased his bothers share in the team taken full control of the Cardinals franchise under his ownership the team was once again relocated to Arizona becoming the Arizona Cardinals in 1994 where they still currently play.

The Cardinals remain owned by the Bidwill's with Bill assuming the role of Chairman, Mike Bidwill the President, Steve Keim the teams General Manager and Kliff Kingsbury the Head Coach. Their current home field is State Farm Stadium where they have played their home games since 2006.

The Cardinals through their years of name changes and relocations have won two NFL League Championships pre-NFL/AFL merger in 1925 and again in 1947. They have won one Conference Championship, seven Division Championships and have appeared in eleven Playoffs. They made it to Super Bowl XLIII in 2008 playing against the Pittsburgh Steelers to whom they lost the title 27 – 23.

They currently hold the NFL record for the first franchise to have lost 700 games since their inception and hold the longest active championship drought of any professional sports team of North America at seventy consecutive seasons.

The Cardinals have had sixteen players inducted into the Pro Football Hall of Fame alongside team owner Charles Bidwell and coaches Jimmy Conzelman, Early "Curly" Lambeau and Joe Stydahar. They only have five retired jersey numbers which include numbers 8 – last worn by Larry Wilson, 40 – last worn by the late Pat Tillman, 77 – last worn by the late Stan Mauldin, 88 – last worn by the late J. V. Cain and 99 – last worn by Marshall Goldberg.

Chicago/St. Louis/Phoenix/Arizona Cardinals Franchise Encyclopedia

Seasons: 100 (1920 to 2019)

Record (W-L-T): 553-753-40

Playoff Record: 7-9

Super Bowls Won: 0 (1 Appearance)

Championships Won*: 2

All-time Passing Leader: Jim Hart 2,590/5,069, 34,639 yds, 209 TD

All-time Rushing Leader: Ottis Anderson 1,858 att, 7,999 yds, 46 TD

All-time Receiving Leader: Larry Fitzgerald 1,303 rec, 16,279 yds, 116 TD

All-time Scoring Leader: Jim Bakken 1,380 points

All-time AV Leader: Jim Hart 136 AV

Winningest Coach: Bruce Arians 49-30-1

JIM HART

TEAMS OF THE NFL

LOS ANGELES RAMS

The Los Angeles Rams were founded in 1936 by Homer Marshman and were called the Cleveland Rams. They came from Cleveland, Ohio and played for the second American Football League that operated between 1936 and 1937 before joining the NFL when the AFL folded at the end of the 1937 season.

In 1937 they played for the NFL in the Western Division with the teams' operations being suspended in 1943 due to a shortage of players during World War II. It began playing again in 1944 where the team continued to play in Cleveland under the name Cleveland Rams.

Following their 1945 NFL Championship victory, the team was moved to Los Angeles in 1946 which paved the way for the All-American Football Conferences team owned by Paul Brown, the Cleveland Browns. The Rams became the only team in the NFL to play the season in another city. It was in 1946 that the team's name was changed to the Los Angeles Rams up until 1944 when the team was once again moved to St Louis becoming the St Louis Rams.

They played in St Louis for twelve seasons before being moved back to Los Angeles at the end of the 2015 season and started playing the 2016 season once again as the Los Angeles Rams for the NFC West Division. During the Rams history, they have won two NFL Championships (1945 and 1951) pre the AFL-NFL merger and one Super Bowl (XXXIV – 1999). They have won seven Conference Championships, twenty Division Championships and appeared in twenty-nine Playoffs.

Their Super Bowl victory was over the Tennessee Titans 13 – 16 and have appeared in one other Super Bowl where they played and lost against the New England Patriots 20 – 17 at the Super Bowl XXXVI in 2001 season.

Carroll Rosenbloom took control of the Rams before the 1972 season becoming the majority shareholder. At the age of 72 in April of 1979, he drowned while swimming at Golden Beach in Florida and left the majority of his shares to his widow Georgia Frontiere who became the first active female majority owner in the NFL. During her tenure as the Rams owner, she was much criticised and bullied for being a woman in a male-dominated league. But in one of her first press conferences after assuming control of the team she soon took control of the situation by saying "There are some who feel there are two different kinds of people – human beings and women".

Upon Georgia's death in 2008 sixty percent of the ownership for the Rams went to her children, son Dale Rosenbloom and daughter Lucia Rodriguez. In August 2010 the team was taken over by Stan Kroenke. The team's current general manager is Les Snead with Head Coach Sean McVay. The team has had seventeen players inducted into the Pro Football Hall of Fame alongside owner Dan Reeves and Head Coach George Allen. The teams eight retired jerseys include numbers 7 – last worn by Bob Waterfield, 28 – last worn by Marshall Faulk, 29 – last worn by Eric Dickerson, 74 – last worn by Merlin Olsen, 75 – last worn by Deacon Jones, 78 – last worn by Jackie Slater, 80 – last worn by Isaac Bruce and 85 – last worn by Jack Youngblood.

Cleveland/St. Louis/LA Rams Franchise Encyclopedia

Seasons: 83 (1937 to 2019)

Record (W-L-T): 568-562-21

Playoff Record: 21-26

Super Bowls Won: 1 (4 Appearances)

Championships Won*: 3

All-time Passing Leader: Jim Everett 1,847/3,277, 23,758 yds, 142 TD

All-time Rushing Leader: Steven Jackson 2,396 att, 10,138 yds, 56 TD

All-time Receiving Leader: Isaac Bruce 942 rec, 14,109 yds, 84 TD

All-time Scoring Leader: Jeff Wilkins 1,223 points

All-time AV Leader: Merlin Olsen 160 AV

Winningest Coach: John Robinson 75-68-0

TEAMS OF THE NFL

SAN FRANCISCO 49ERS

Established in June of 1946 by Tony Morabito, who was an owner of a successful lumber hauling company. He and his brother Vic co-owned the team until Tony died of a heart attack whilst watching the 49ers play the Chicago Bears on the 27 October 1957. His majority shares were passed to his widow Josephine.

The 49ers started the Pro Football playing for the All-American Football Conference (AAFC) after Morabito had been rejected several times by the NFL for an expansion team. They played their first official season in 1946 to become one of the first major league professional sports teams on the Pacific Coast and first major sports franchise in San Fransico.

After the AAFC Folded at the end of the 1949 season the 49ers joined the NFL playing in the Coastal Division where they played until the AFL-NFL merger in 1970 where they play as a member team of the NFC West Division. Their home stadium is currently Levi's stadium where they have played their home games since 2014. They started their early years playing at Kezar Stadium up until 1970 after which they moved to Candlestick Park until 2013.

The San Fransico 49ers are one of the most successful teams in the history of the NFL having won five Super Bowls championships (XVI – 1981, XIX – 1984, XXIII – 1988, XXIV 1989 and XXIX in 1994). They have appeared in the League Playoffs fifty times, won six Conference Championships and nineteen Division Championships. They set many NFL records including most field goals in a season – 44, fewest turnovers in a season – 10, most touchdowns in a Super Bowl, most consecutive seasons leading league scoring between 1992 through to 1995. They have also set the NFL record for most consecutive games scored between 1979 and 2004 as well as most consecutive road games won – 18.

The team was ranked as the tenth most valuable sports team in the world and Forbes Magazine ranks them as the fourth most valuable team in the NFL with a worth of $3 billion.

The 49ers were famous for their "Million Dollar Backfield" during the 1950s which consisted of players who are mostly all currently listed in the Pro Football Hall of Fame to become the only full-house backfield to be inducted into the Pro Football Hall of Fame. These players were running backs Hugh McElhenny, Joe Perry and John Henry Johnson along with quarterback J. A. Tittle.

In 1960 they became the first team to use the "shotgun formation" which was devised by their then head coach Red Hickey. This formation enabled the 49ers to get the edge over the Baltimore Colts and win the game.

In 1977 the widows of the late Morabito brothers decided to sell their shares to Edward DeBartolo who saw the team take five Super Bowl Championships during his time in ownership. In 2000 DeBartolo's Daughter and her husband gained the majority of the 49ers shares which she has since given over to her son Jed York. The current president of the team is Al Guido, General Manager is John Lynch and their Head Coach is Kyle Shanahan.

San Francisco 49ers Franchise Encyclopedia

Seasons: 74 (1946 to 2019)

Record (W-L-T): 570-486-16

Playoff Record: 31-21

Super Bowls Won: 5 (6 Appearances)

Championships Won*: 5

All-time Passing Leader: Joe Montana 2,929/4,600, 35,124 yds, 244 TD

All-time Rushing Leader: Frank Gore 2,442 att, 11,073 yds, 64 TD

All-time Receiving Leader: Jerry Rice 1,281 rec, 19,247 yds, 176 TD

All-time Scoring Leader: Jerry Rice 1,130 points

All-time AV Leader: Jerry Rice 215 AV

Winningest Coach: George Seifert 98-30-0

TEAMS OF THE NFL

SEATTLE SEAHAWKS

A group of Seattle business and community leaders were awarded an NFL expansion team in 1974 as part of the NFL's expansion move to expand the league from twenty-six to twenty-eight teams. John Thompson, who was a former NFL Executive Director was appointed the General Manager of the new team. In 1975 a public naming contest was held from which the name Seahawk won from over 20,000 entries.

Former assistant coach for the Minnesota Vikings, Jack Patera was hired by John Thompson as the first head coach for the new Seattle Seahawks team in 1976. They played their first season in 1976 where they played for the NFC West. They were switched to the AFC West division for 1977 through to the end of the 2001 season. They were once again switched back to the NFC West Division in 2002 where they currently play making them the only team in the NFL to have switched conferences twice.

Their initial home field was Kingdome from 1976 to 1999 although a few of their home games were played a the Husky stadium in 1994 due to repairs to the Kingdome. In 2000 they moved to the Husky Stadium, they moved to their current home stadium CenturyLink Field in 2002. Their fan base has been referred to as the "12th man" and is some of the loudest fans having twice set the Guinness World Record for being the loudest crowd at a sporting event. Their first record-setting cheers were recorded as 136.6 decibels which were a game against the 49ers and the 137.6 decibels during a Monday Night Football game which the Panthers played against the New Orleans Saints.

Seattle Seahawks Franchise Encyclopedia

Seasons: 44 (1976 to 2019)

Record (W-L-T): 344-331-1

Playoff Record: 16-16

Super Bowls Won: 1
(3 Appearances)

Championships Won*: 1

All-time Passing Leader:
Matt Hasselbeck 2,559/4,250, 29,434 yds, 174 TD

All-time Rushing Leader:
Shaun Alexander 2,176 att, 9,429 yds, 100 TD

All-time Receiving Leader:
Steve Largent 819 rec, 13,089 yds, 100 TD

All-time Scoring Leader:
Norm Johnson 810 points

All-time AV Leader:
Steve Largent 140 AV

Winningest Coach:
Pete Carroll 89-54-1

As the only NFL franchise based in the Pacific Northwest they draw their fan base from a wide geographical area including Idaho, Montana, Oregon, Alaska and even some parts of Canada such as Alberta, Saskatchewan and British Columbia. Since they have played as a Pro Football team, they have won three Conference Championships, ten Division Championships and appeared in 17 Playoffs.

The Panthers have played in three Super Bowls only winning one of them which was the Super Bowl XLVIII in 2013 season where they beat the Denver Broncos for the title 43 – 8. Super Bowl XL in the 2005 season they played against the Pittsburgh Steelers and lost 21 – 10. Super Bowl XLIX in the 2014 season had the Panthers playing the New England Patriots for the title but they were defeated by a narrow margin 28 – 24.

In 1996 the current owner of the Seahawks, Ken Behring was threatening to move the team to South Carolina. Instead, they were bought by billionaire and co-founder of Microsoft Paul Allen. The team is still owned by Allen's estate after he died in 2018 with his sister Jody Allen as the executor, Chuck Arnold as the teams President, John Schneider as their General Manager and Pete Carroll as their head coach.

The team have five retired jerseys which are number 12 which has been dedicated to their fans since 1976, 45 – last worn by Kenny Easley, 71 – last worn by Walter Jones, 80 – last worn by Steve Largent and then Jerry rice for the 2004 season and number 96 – last work by the late Cortez Kennedy. Ten of the Panthers players have been inducted into the Pro Football Hall of Fame.

STEVE LARGENT

STADIUMS OF THE NFL

AT&T Stadium

AT&T Stadium, formerly Cowboys Stadium, is a retractable roof stadium in Arlington, Texas. It serves as the home of the Dallas Cowboys of the National Football League (NFL) and was completed on May 27, 2009. It is also the home of the Cotton Bowl Classic and the Big 12 Championship Game. The facility, owned by the city of Arlington, is also be used for a variety of other activities such as concerts, basketball games, college and high school football contests, rodeos and motocross and Spartan races. It replaced the partially covered Texas Stadium, which served as the Cowboys' home from 1971 through the 2008 season.

The stadium is sometimes referred to as "Jerry World" after Dallas Cowboys owner Jerry Jones, who originally envisioned it as a large entertainment mecca. The stadium seats 80,000, making it the fourth largest stadium in the NFL by seating capacity. The maximum capacity of the stadium with standing room is 105,000. The record attendance for an NFL game was set in 2009 with a crowd of 105,121. The Party Pass (open areas) sections are behind seats in each end zone and on a series of six elevated platforms connected by stairways. It also has the world's 29th largest high definition video screen, which hangs from 20-yard line to 20-yard line.

Arrowhead Stadium

Arrowhead Stadium is located in Kansas City, Missouri. It primarily serves as the home venue of the Kansas City Chiefs of the National Football League (NFL).

It is part of the Truman Sports Complex with adjacent Kauffman Stadium, the home of the Kansas City Royals of Major League Baseball (MLB). Arrowhead Stadium has a seating capacity of 76,416, making it the 27th largest stadium in the United States and the sixth largest NFL stadium. It is also the largest sports facility by capacity in the state of Missouri. A $375 million renovation was completed in 2010.

When the Dallas Texans relocated to Kansas City in 1963 and were renamed the Kansas City Chiefs, they played home games at Municipal Stadium, which they shared with the Kansas City Athletics of Major League Baseball. The A's left for Oakland after the 1967 season and were replaced by the Kansas City Royals in 1969. Municipal Stadium, built in 1923 and mostly rebuilt in 1955, seated approximately 35,000 for football. As part of the AFL–NFL merger announced in 1966, NFL stadiums would be required to seat no fewer than 50,000 people. The City of Kansas City was unable to find a suitable location for a new stadium, so Jackson County stepped in and offered a location on the eastern edge of Kansas City near the interchange of Interstate 70 and Interstate 435.

Voters approved a $102 million bond issue in 1967 to build a new sports complex with two stadiums. The original design called for construction of side-by-side baseball and football stadiums with a common roof that would roll between them. The design proved to be more complicated and expensive than originally thought and so was scrapped in favor of the current open-air configuration. The two-stadium complex concept was the first of its kind. The Chiefs staff, led by team general manager Jack Steadman, helped develop the complex.

STADIUMS OF THE NFL

Bank of America Stadium

Bank of America Stadium is a 75,523-seat football stadium located on 33 acres (13 ha) in uptown Charlotte, North Carolina. It is the home facility and headquarters of the Carolina Panthers. The stadium opened in 1996 as Ericsson Stadium before Bank of America purchased the naming rights in 2004. Former Panthers president Danny Morrison called it "A classic American stadium" due to its bowl design and other features.

In addition to the Panthers, the stadium hosts the annual Belk Bowl, which features teams from the Atlantic Coast Conference (ACC) and the Southeastern Conference (SEC), and was supposed to host the annual ACC Championship Game through to at least 2019. The game was moved in 2016 but reinstated in 2017. The largest crowd to ever attend a football game at the stadium was on September 9, 2018 when 74,532 fans watched the Panthers defeat the Dallas Cowboys 16-8.

In addition to hosting every Panthers home game since 1996, Bank of America Stadium has hosted seven playoff games. Carolina has also had over 150 consecutive sellouts at the stadium starting with the 2002 season.

Broncos Stadium at Mile High

Broncos Stadium at Mile High, previously known as Invesco Field at Mile High and Sports Authority Field at Mile High, and commonly known as Mile High, New Mile High or Mile High Stadium, is located in Denver, Colorado, named Mile High due to the city's elevation of 5,280 feet (1,610 m). The primary tenant is the Denver Broncos of the National Football League (NFL). It opened in 2001 to replace Mile High Stadium and was largely paid for by taxpayers. Invesco paid $120 million for the original naming rights, before Sports Authority secured them in 2011.

Despite its sponsor's liquidation and closure in 2016, the Sports Authority name remained on the stadium for two years afterwards because of regulatory hurdles. Nevertheless, the Broncos announced on January 2, 2018 that the stadium's exterior signage would be removed. The stadium took on its current name on a temporary basis on June 20, 2018 after the city's stadium authority approved the change, hoping to resell naming rights.

On September 10, 2001, the stadium hosted its first regular season NFL game, in which the Broncos defeated the New York Giants 31–20. In a pre-game ceremony, Broncos legends John Elway, Steve Atwater, Randy Gradishar, Haven Moses, Billy Thompson, Floyd Little, Dennis Smith, and Karl Mecklenburg helped to "Move the Thunder" from the old Mile High Stadium to the new home of the Broncos.

The stadium has hosted several NFL playoff games. It hosted the 2005 AFC Divisional playoff game, in which Denver defeated the New England Patriots 27–13. The following week, it hosted the AFC Championship Game, which the Broncos lost to the Pittsburgh Steelers, 34–17. On January 8, 2012, the stadium hosted its third NFL playoff game, an AFC Wild Card playoff game against the Steelers. The Broncos won in overtime, 29–23. On January 12, 2013, the stadium hosted its fourth NFL playoff game, an AFC Divisional playoff game against the Baltimore Ravens. The Broncos lost to the Ravens 38–35 in double overtime.

On October 29, 2007, a record crowd of 77,160 watched the Broncos lose to the Green Bay Packers 19–13 on Monday Night Football on the first play from scrimmage in overtime.

On November 26, 2009, it hosted its first Thanksgiving game, when the Broncos took on the Giants. The game was televised on NFL Network, which the Broncos won by a final score of 26–6. On January 19, 2014, the Broncos defeated the Patriots in the AFC Championship Game, 26–16 in front of 77,110 fans in attendance, advancing to their first Super Bowl since they began play in the new stadium. On January 17, 2016, the Broncos defeated the Steelers in the AFC Divisional playoffs, 23–16 in front of 77,100, advancing to the AFC Championship Game for the 10th time in franchise history. On January 24, 2016, the Broncos defeated the Patriots in the AFC Championship Game, 20–18 in front of 77,100, advancing to Super Bowl 50, which they won two weeks later.

CenturyLink Field

CenturyLink Field is a multi-purpose stadium located in Seattle, Washington and is the home field for the Seattle Seahawks and Seattle Sounders FC of Major League Soccer (MLS). Originally called Seahawks Stadium, it became Qwest Field in June 2004, when telecommunications carrier Qwest acquired the naming rights. It received its current name in June 2011 after Qwest's acquisition by CenturyLink. It is a modern facility with views of the Downtown Seattle skyline and can seat 69,000 people for NFL games and 37,722 for most MLS matches. The complex also includes the Event Center with the Washington Music Theater (WaMu Theater), a parking garage, and a public plaza. The venue hosts concerts, trade shows, and consumer shows along with sporting events. Located within a mile (1.6 km) of Downtown Seattle, the stadium is accessible by multiple freeways and forms of mass transit.

The stadium was built between 2000 and 2002 on the site of the Kingdome after voters approved funding for the construction in a statewide election held in June 1997. This vote created the Washington State Public Stadium Authority to oversee public ownership of the venue. The owner of the Seahawks, Paul Allen, formed First & Goal Inc. to develop and operate the new facilities. Allen was closely involved in the design process and emphasized the importance of an open-air venue with an intimate atmosphere.

The crowd is notoriously loud during Seahawks games. It has twice held the Guinness World Record for loudest crowd roar at an outdoor stadium, first at 136.6 decibels in 2013, followed by a measurement of 137.6 decibels in 2014. The noise has contributed to the team's home field advantage with an increase in false start (movement by an offensive player prior to the play) and delay of game (failure of the offense to snap the ball prior to the play clock expiring) penalties against visiting teams. The stadium was the first in the NFL to implement a FieldTurf artificial field. Numerous college and high school American football games have also been played at the stadium.

Dignity Health Sports Park

Dignity Health Sports Park, formerly the Home Depot Center and StubHub Center, is a multiple-use sports complex located on the campus of California State University, Dominguez Hills in Carson, California that consists of a soccer stadium, a separate tennis stadium, a track and field facility, and a velodrome: VELO Sports Center. It is approximately fourteen miles (23 km) south of downtown Los Angeles and its primary tenant is the LA Galaxy of Major League Soccer (MLS). It is also the temporary home of the Los Angeles Chargers.

Opened in 2003, the $150 million complex was developed and is operated by the Anschutz Entertainment Group. With a seating capacity of 27,000, it is the largest soccer-specific stadium in the U.S. and the second-largest among its kind in MLS, after Canadian Toronto FC's BMO Field. In addition to hosting LA Galaxy games since its opening, the stadium also served as the home of the now-defunct Chivas USA MLS team from 2005 to 2014.

The stadium became the temporary home of the Los Angeles Chargers beginning in 2017 – making it the smallest NFL stadium – until the completion of the Los Angeles Stadium at Hollywood Park in 2020, which they will then share with the Los Angeles Rams. During the 2018 Los Angeles Chargers season, while the Chargers played in the stadium, the facility was named ROKiT Field at StubHub Center; ROKiT's naming rights to the football field are part of a "multi-year" agreement.

During its first decade, the stadium's sponsor was hardware retailer The Home Depot. In 2013, the title sponsor became the online ticket marketplace StubHub. In 2019, the name sponsor became healthcare provider Dignity Health.

FedExField

FedExField was built as a replacement for the Redskins' prior venue, Robert F. Kennedy Memorial Stadium in Washington, D.C. In 1994 Jack Kent Cooke sought to build a new stadium on the grounds adjacent to Laurel Park Racecourse along Whiskey Bottom and Brock Bridge roads. Lack of parking facilities and support prompted a second site selection.

The stadium opened in 1997 as Jack Kent Cooke Stadium, in honor of the recently deceased owner of the team, and the stadium site was known as Raljon from the first names of Cooke's sons – "Ralph" and "John". Notably, Cooke was able to register Raljon with the United States Postal Service as a legal alternate address for the 20785 zip code of Landover, Maryland, where the stadium is located, and went to some lengths to require media to use Raljon in datelines from the stadium. This ended when Daniel Snyder bought the Redskins from the Cooke estate, and the Redskins now give the stadium's address as Landover.

After Snyder's purchase, the stadium's naming rights were sold to FedEx in November 1999 for an average of $7.6 million per year. The waiting list for Redskins season tickets was reportedly over 160,000 names long. However, according to The Washington Post, Redskins ticket office employees improperly sold tickets directly to ticket brokers for several years before the practice was discovered in 2009.

Although the Redskins have never sold out the entire stadium, the team has not had a game blacked out on local television since 1972 (when home game broadcasts were banned outright) because it does not count "premium club level seating" when calculating sellouts (their sellout streak dates to 1965, eight years before the new blackout rules were implemented).

From 2004 to 2010 Redskins fans set the NFL regular-season home paid attendance records. In 2005 the team drew a record 716,998 fans overall. The December 30, 2007, 27–6 win against the Dallas Cowboys was the most watched game in Redskins history, with 90,910 fans in the stands to see Washington clinch a playoff spot.

On January 8, 2000, the Washington Redskins defeated the Detroit Lions 27–13 in the first NFL playoff game at FedExField. On December 29, 2002, the Redskins defeated the rival Dallas Cowboys, 20–14. This game was Darrell Green's final game. He played 20 seasons with the Redskins. The game also broke a 10-game losing streak to the Cowboys.

FirstEnergy Stadium

FirstEnergy Stadium is located on the site of Cleveland Stadium, commonly called Cleveland Municipal Stadium, a multipurpose facility built in 1931 that served as the Browns' home field from their inception in 1946 through the 1995 season. During the 1995 season, owner Art Modell announced his plans to move the team to Baltimore, which resulted in legal action from the city of Cleveland and Browns season ticket holders. The day after the announcement was made, voters in Cuyahoga County approved an extension of the original 1990 sin tax on alcohol and tobacco products to fund renovations to Cleveland Stadium. Eventually, as part of the agreement between Modell, the city of Cleveland, and the NFL, the city agreed to tear down Cleveland Stadium and build a new stadium on the same site using the sin tax funds. Modell agreed to leave the Browns name, colors, and history in Cleveland and create a new identity for his franchise, eventually becoming the Baltimore Ravens, while the NFL agreed to reactivate the Browns by 1999 through expansion or relocation of another team. Demolition on the old stadium began in November 1996 and was completed in early 1997. Debris from the former stadium was submerged in Lake Erie and now serves as an artificial reef.

Ground was broken for the new stadium on May 15, 1997, and it opened in July 1999. The first event was a preseason game between the Browns and the Minnesota Vikings on August 21, followed the next week by a preseason game against the Chicago Bears. The first regular-season Browns game at the stadium was played the evening of September 12, 1999, a 43–0 loss to the Pittsburgh Steelers.

Since 2011, the stadium has been referred to by some as the "Factory of Sadness", a name that was first coined that year by comedian and Browns fan Mike Polk. Polk made a video outside the stadium in which he complains about the team's futility. Through the 2018 season, FirstEnergy Stadium is the only NFL venue that has yet to host a postseason game of any kind. The Browns are one of five teams who have yet to host a home playoff game in their respective stadium, along with the Atlanta Falcons, San Francisco 49ers, Detroit Lions, and New York Jets. These teams, however, have hosted the Super Bowl at their respective stadiums, while the Jets' home, MetLife Stadium, has also hosted a New York Giants home playoff game.

Ford Field

Ford Field is a multi-purpose domed stadium located in Downtown Detroit. It primarily serves as the home of the Detroit Lions of the National Football League (NFL), as well as the annual Quick Lane Bowl college football bowl game, state championship football games for the MHSAA, and, as of 2018, the MHSAA State Wrestling Championships. The regular seating capacity is approximately 65,000, though it is expandable up to 70,000 for football and 80,000 for basketball. The naming rights were purchased by the Ford Motor Company at $40 million over 20 years; the Ford family holds a controlling interest in the company, and a member of the Ford family has controlled ownership of the Lions franchise since 1963.

The stadium's design incorporates a former Hudson's warehouse, which was constructed in the 1920s.

The presence of the warehouse allows for a seating arrangement that's unique among professional American football stadiums. The majority of suites are located in the warehouse along the stadium's southern sideline, as are the lounges that serve the premium club seats on that side of the field. The bulk of the grandstand seats are located along the northern sideline and both end-lines, with gaps in the stadium's upper half at the southwest and southeast corners. The upper deck on the stadium's northern sideline also contains one level of suites and a smaller section of club seating. A similar design was implemented at the renovated Soldier Field, albeit with the use of a new structure (as opposed to an existing building) to house four levels of suites.

Unlike most domed stadiums, Ford Field allows a large amount of natural light to reach the field, thanks to immense skylights and large glass windows at the open corners. The windows along the ceiling are frosted to mimic the automotive factories that are prevalent in Metro Detroit. The south entrance provides the seating bowl and concourse with sunlight year-round and also offers fans a view of downtown Detroit. To prevent the stadium from becoming an overly imposing presence in the Detroit skyline, the playing field is 45 feet below street level, similar to the design at adjacent Comerica Park.

Ford Field is one of the few venues in the NFL that has end zones in the east and the west. There is no NFL rule for field construction regarding sunlight distracting players on the field. The east–west end zone design accommodated the Hudson warehouse location. The natural light is not a distraction to the players in a day game, because the light only reaches as far as the sidelines, leaving the field still properly lit with the combination of artificial stadium lighting and sunlight.

In 2017, Ford Field underwent its first major renovation. The $100 million renovation included new video boards, a new sound system, updated suites, and the renovation of multiple restaurants, clubs, and bars on the property.

Gillette Stadium

Gillette Stadium is located in Foxborough, Massachusetts, 28 miles (45 km) southwest of downtown Boston and 20 miles (32 km) northeast of downtown Providence, Rhode Island. It serves as the home stadium and administrative offices for both the New England Patriots of the National Football League (NFL) and the New England Revolution of Major League Soccer (MLS). In 2012, it also became the home stadium for the football program of the University of Massachusetts (UMass), while on-campus Warren McGuirk Alumni Stadium was undergoing renovations. Gillette will continue to host higher attended home games.

The facility opened in 2002, replacing Foxboro Stadium. The seating capacity is 65,878, including 5,876 club seats and 89 luxury suites. The stadium is owned and operated by Kraft Sports Group, a subsidiary of The Kraft Group, the company through which businessman Robert Kraft owns the Patriots and Revolution.

The stadium was originally known as CMGI Field before the naming rights were bought by Gillette after the "dot-com" bust. Although Gillette was acquired by Procter & Gamble (P&G) in 2005, the stadium retains the Gillette name because P&G has continued to use the Gillette brand name and because the Gillette company was founded in the Boston area. Gillette and the Patriots jointly announced in September 2010 that their partnership, which includes naming rights to the stadium, will extend through the 2031 season. Additionally, uBid (until April 2003 a wholly owned subsidiary of CMGI) as of 2009 continues to sponsor one of the main entrance gates to the stadium.

The Town of Foxborough approved plans for the stadium's construction on December 6, 1999, and work on the stadium began on March 24, 2000. The first official event was a New England Revolution soccer game on May 11, 2002. The Rolling Stones played at Gillette Stadium on September 5, 2002 on the band's Licks Tour. Jeremiah Freed was the first band to play at the WBCN river rave on June 9, 2002 making them the first band to ever play Gillette Stadium. Grand opening ceremonies were held four days later on September 9 when the Patriots unveiled their Super Bowl XXXVI championship banner before a Monday Night Football game against the Pittsburgh Steelers.

The Patriots have sold out every home game since moving to the stadium—preseason, regular season, and playoffs. This streak dates back to the 1994 season, while the team was still at Foxboro Stadium. By September 2016 this streak was 231 straight games.

Hard Rock Stadium

Hard Rock Stadium is a multipurpose football stadium located in Miami Gardens, Florida. It is the home stadium of the Miami Dolphins. Hard Rock Stadium also plays host to the Miami Hurricanes football team during their regular season. The facility also hosts the Orange Bowl, an annual college football bowl game. It was the home to the Florida Marlins of Major League Baseball (MLB) from 1993 to 2011. From 2019, the stadium is home to the Miami Open tennis tournament, played in March.

The stadium has hosted five Super Bowls (XXIII, XXIX, XXXIII, XLI and XLIV), the 2010 Pro Bowl, two World Series (1997 and 2003), four BCS National Championship Games (2001, 2005, 2009, 2013), the second round of the 2009 World Baseball Classic, and WrestleMania XXVIII. The stadium will host Super Bowl LIV in 2020 and the College Football Playoff National Championship in 2021.

The facility opened in 1987 as Joe Robbie Stadium and has been known by a number of names since: Pro Player Park, Pro Player Stadium, Dolphins Stadium, Dolphin Stadium, Land Shark Stadium, and Sun Life Stadium. In August 2016 the team sold the naming rights to Hard Rock Cafe Inc. for $250 million over 18 years.

For their first 21 seasons, the Miami Dolphins played at the Orange Bowl. Joe Robbie, the team's founder, led the financing campaign to build a new home for the team. He believed it was only a matter of time before a Major League Baseball team came to South Florida. At his request, the stadium was built so only minimal renovations would be necessary to ready it for a baseball team. Most notably, the field was made somewhat wider than is normally the case for an NFL stadium. The wide field also made it fairly easy to convert the stadium for soccer.

Because of this design decision, the first row of seats was 90 ft (27 m) from the sideline in a football configuration, considerably more distant than the first row of seats in most football stadiums (the closest seats at the new Soldier Field, for instance, are 55 ft (17 m) from the sideline at the 50-yard line). This resulted in a less intimate venue for football compared to other football facilities built around this time, as well as to the Orange Bowl.

At the time it opened in 1987, the stadium was located in an unincorporated area within Miami-Dade County, and had a Miami address. Miami Gardens was incorporated on May 13, 2003.

Heinz Field

Heinz Field is a stadium located in the North Shore neighborhood of Pittsburgh, Pennsylvania. It primarily serves as the home to the Pittsburgh Steelers and the Pittsburgh Panthers of the National Collegiate Athletic Association (NCAA). The stadium opened in 2001, after the controlled implosion of the teams' previous stadium, Three Rivers Stadium. The stadium is named for the locally based H. J. Heinz Company, which purchased the naming rights in 2001. It hosted the 2011 NHL Winter Classic between the Pittsburgh Penguins and Washington Capitals on January 1, 2011. On September 10, 2016, it hosted the Keystone Classic, which featured a renewal of the Penn State-Pitt football rivalry, setting a new attendance record at 69,983 people. In 2017 it hosted the Coors Light Stadium Series game featuring the Pittsburgh Penguins and Philadelphia Flyers.

Funded in conjunction with PNC Park and the David L. Lawrence Convention Center, the $281 million stadium stands along the Ohio River, on the Northside of Pittsburgh in the North Shore neighborhood. The stadium was designed with the city of Pittsburgh's history of steel production in mind, which led to the inclusion of 12,000 tons of steel into construction. Ground for the stadium was broken in June 1999 and the first football game was hosted in September 2001. The stadium's natural grass surface has been criticized throughout its history, but Steelers ownership has kept the grass after lobbying from players and coaches. Attendance for the 68,400 seat stadium has sold out for every Steelers home game, a streak which dates back to 1972 (a year before local telecasts of sold out home games were permitted in the NFL). A collection of memorabilia from the Steelers and Panthers of the past can be found in the Great Hall.

The quickest score in NFL history occurred on September 8, 2013, in the Steelers season opener against the Tennessee Titans, when the Steelers scored a safety on the opening kickoff three seconds into the game. Darius Reynaud of the Titans fielded the kickoff and took a short step backwards (into the south end zone) for what was ruled to be a safety, not a touchback, because the ball was not in the end zone when it was fielded. The Steelers, however, lost the game 16-9, which was also their first home opener loss since Heinz Field opened.

The longest NFL field goal ever kicked in Heinz Field is 53 yards. Dallas Cowboys kicker Dan Bailey first set the record in 2016. That record was tied on November 26, 2017 by Pittsburgh Steelers kicker Chris Boswell in a game-winning effort over the Green Bay Packers with 4 seconds remaining in the game, resulting in a 31-28 win. In collegiate play, University of Pittsburgh kicker Alex Kessman kicked a 55-yard field goal against the Syracuse Orange on October 6, 2018.

Lambeau Field

Lambeau Field is located in Green Bay, Wisconsin. The home field of the Green Bay Packers, it opened in 1957 as City Stadium, replacing the original City Stadium at East High School as the Packers' home field. Informally known as New City Stadium for its first eight seasons, it was renamed in August 1965 in memory of Packers founder, player, and long-time head coach, Curly Lambeau, who had died two months earlier.

The stadium's street address has been 1265 Lombardi Avenue since August 1968, when Highland Avenue was renamed in honor of former head coach Vince Lombardi. It sits on a block bounded by Lombardi Avenue (north); Oneida Street (east); Stadium Drive and Valley View Road (south); and Ridge Road (west). The playing field at the stadium has a conventional north-south alignment, at an elevation of 640 feet (195 m) above sea level.

The stadium completed its latest renovation in the summer of 2013 with the addition of 7,000 seats high in the south end zone. About 5,400 of the new seating is general, while the remaining 1,600 seats are club or terrace suite seating. With a capacity of 81,441, Lambeau Field is the fifth-largest stadium in the NFL with standing room, but is fourth in normal capacity. It is now the largest venue in the state, edging out Camp Randall Stadium (80,321) at the University of Wisconsin in Madison.

Lambeau Field is the oldest continually operating NFL stadium. In 2007, the Packers completed their 51st season at Lambeau, breaking the all-time NFL record set by the Chicago Bears at Wrigley Field (1921–70). (While Soldier Field in Chicago is older, it was not the home of the Bears until 1971.) Only the Boston Red Sox at Fenway Park and the Chicago Cubs at Wrigley have longer active home-field tenures in American professional sports.

Levi's Stadium

Levi's Stadium is located in Santa Clara, California, in the Bay Area. It has served as the home venue for the National Football League's San Francisco 49ers since 2014. The stadium is located approximately 40 miles (64 km) south of San Francisco and is named for Levi Strauss & Co., which purchased naming rights in 2013.

In 2006, the 49ers proposed constructing a new stadium at Candlestick Point in San Francisco, the site of their existing home, Candlestick Park. The project, which included plans for retail space and housing improvements, was claimed to be of great potential benefit to the nearby historically blighted neighborhood of Hunters Point. After negotiations with the city of San Francisco fell through, the 49ers focused their attention on a site adjacent to their administrative offices and training facility in Santa Clara.

In June 2010, Santa Clara voters approved a measure authorizing the creation of the tax-exempt Santa Clara Stadium Authority to build and own the new football stadium and for the city to lease land to the authority. A construction loan raised from private investors was secured in December 2011, allowing construction to start in April 2012. Levi's Stadium opened on July 17, 2014.

Levi's Stadium has been the site of the Pac-12 Football Championship Game since 2014. Previously, that game was played on the home field of the division winner possessing the better record. Levi's Stadium hosted Super Bowl 50 on February 7, 2016. It also hosted Alabama and Clemson for the 2019 College Football Playoff National Championship.

Lincoln Financial Field

Lincoln Financial Field is located in Philadelphia, Pennsylvania. It serves as the home stadium of the Philadelphia Eagles of the National Football League and the Temple Owls football team of Temple University. It is located in South Philadelphia on Pattison Avenue between 11th and South Darien streets, also alongside I-95 as part of the South Philadelphia Sports Complex. It has a seating capacity of 69,176. Many locals refer to the stadium simply as "The Linc".

The stadium opened on August 3, 2003 after two years of construction that began on May 7, 2001, replacing Veterans Stadium. While total seating capacity is similar to that of "The Vet", the new stadium contains double the number of luxury and wheelchair-accessible seats, along with more modern services. The field's construction included several light emitting diode (LED) video displays, as well as more than 624 feet (190 m) of LED ribbon boards.

Naming rights were sold in June 2002 to the Lincoln Financial Group, for a sum of $139.6 million over 21 years. Together, the City of Philadelphia and the State of Pennsylvania contributed approximately $188 million to the stadium construction. Additional construction funding was raised from the sale of Stadium Builder's Licenses to Eagles season ticket holders.

The Army–Navy football game is frequently played at the stadium due to Philadelphia being located halfway between both service academies, the stadium being able to house the large crowds in attendance, and the historic nature of the city. Temple University's Division I college football team also plays their home games at Lincoln Financial Field, paying the Eagles $1 million a year to do so. The Philadelphia Union of Major League Soccer have played exhibition games here against high-profile international clubs when their stadium Talen Energy Stadium does not provide adequate seating. The stadium also plays host to several soccer games each year. It has also played host to the NCAA lacrosse national championship three times, in 2005, 2006, and 2013 respectively.

In late spring 2013, the Eagles announced that there would be some major upgrades to Lincoln Financial Field over the next two years. The total project estimate was valued at over $125 million. The upgrades included seating expansion, two new HD video boards, upgraded amenities, WiFi, and two new connecting bridges for upper levels. These upgrades were decided upon after research from season ticket holders, advisory boards, and fan focus groups. The majority of these changes, including WiFi (which would accommodate 45,000 users and have coverage over the entire stadium), were completed by the 2013 home opener. The upgraded sound systems and video boards were finished for the 2014 season.

Los Angeles Memorial Coliseum

The Los Angeles Memorial Coliseum is located in the Exposition Park neighborhood of Los Angeles, California. Conceived as a hallmark of civic pride, the Coliseum was commissioned in 1921 as a memorial to L.A. veterans of World War I. Completed in 1923, it will be the first stadium to have hosted the Summer Olympics three times: 1932, 1984, and 2028. It was declared a National Historic Landmark on July 27, 1984, the day before the opening ceremony of the 1984 Summer Olympics.

The stadium serves as the home to the University of Southern California (USC) Trojans football team of the Pac-12 Conference. It is also the temporary home of the Los Angeles Rams of the National Football League. The Coliseum was home to the Rams from 1946 to 1979, when they moved to Anaheim Stadium in Anaheim. The Coliseum is serving as their home stadium again until the completion of Los Angeles Stadium at Hollywood Park in Inglewood. The facility had a permanent seating capacity of 93,607 for USC football and Rams games, making it the largest football stadium in the Pac-12 Conference and the NFL.

USC, which operates and manages the Coliseum, began a major renovation of the stadium in early 2018. During the renovation project the seating capacity will be 78,467 and will be 77,500 upon completion in 2019. The $270 million project is scheduled to be completed by the 2019 football season and is the first major upgrade of the stadium in twenty years. The project includes replacing the seating along with the addition of luxury boxes and club suites. Naming rights were granted to United Airlines but following some concerns expressed by veterans groups and the new president of the Coliseum Commission, the naming rights are in limbo. United Airlines did not approve of any change from United Airlines Memorial Coliseum and suggested that they were willing to step away from the deal.

From 1959 to 2016, the Los Angeles Memorial Sports Arena was located adjacent to the Coliseum; the Sports Arena was closed in March 2016 and demolished. Banc of California Stadium, a soccer-specific stadium and home of Major League Soccer's Los Angeles FC, was constructed on the former Sports Arena site and opened in April 2018.

The stadium also was the temporary home of the Los Angeles Dodgers of Major League Baseball from 1958 to 1961 and was the host venue for games 3, 4, and 5 of the 1959 World Series. It was the site of the First AFL-NFL World Championship Game, later called Super Bowl I, and Super Bowl VII. Additionally, it has served as a home field for a number of other teams, including the Los Angeles Raiders of the NFL, and UCLA Bruins football.

Lucas Oil Stadium

Lucas Oil Stadium is a multi-purpose stadium in Downtown Indianapolis, Indiana. It replaced the RCA Dome as the home field of the NFL's Indianapolis Colts and opened on August 16, 2008. The stadium was constructed to allow the removal of the RCA Dome and expansion of the Indiana Convention Center on its site. The stadium is on the south side of South Street, a block south of the former site of the RCA Dome. In 2006, prior to the stadium's construction, Lucas Oil Products secured the naming rights for the stadium at a cost of $122 million over 20 years. The venue also serves as the current home for the United Soccer League's Indy Eleven.

The architectural firm HKS, Inc. was responsible for the stadium's design, with Walter P Moore working as the Structural Engineer of Record. The stadium features a retractable roof and window wall, thus allowing the Colts and the Eleven to play both indoors and outdoors. The field surface was originally FieldTurf but was replaced in 2018 with Shaw Sports Momentum Pro. The exterior of the new stadium is faced with a reddish-brown brick trimmed with Indiana limestone, similar to several other sports venues in the area, including Bankers Life Fieldhouse, Hinkle Fieldhouse, and the Fairgrounds Coliseum.

Lucas Oil Stadium has a seating capacity of 67,000 and covers approximately 1.8 million square feet (170,000 m2). The stadium offers 139 suites, two club lounges, two exhibit halls and 12 meeting rooms. There are also 360-degree ribbon boards and two 53-foot (16 m) tall high definition video boards. An underground walkway directly connects the stadium to the Indiana Convention Center.

M&T Bank Stadium

M&T Bank Stadium is located in Baltimore, Maryland. It is the home of the Baltimore Ravens. The stadium is immediately adjacent to Oriole Park at Camden Yards, the home of the Baltimore Orioles. Often referred to as "Ravens Stadium", M&T Bank Stadium officially opened in 1998, and is currently one of the most praised stadiums in the NFL for fan amenities, ease of access, concessions and other facilities.

The stadium was originally known as Ravens Stadium at Camden Yards, until PSINet acquired the naming rights in 1999, naming it PSINet Stadium. It then reverted to Ravens Stadium in 2002 when PSINet filed for bankruptcy. M&T Bank bought the naming rights in 2003 and signed a 15-year, $75 million contract with the Ravens, which was brokered by Team Services, LLC. The naming rights deal for M&T Bank Stadium was renewed for $60M over 10 years in 2014, extending the name through 2027.

Ground was broken for the new stadium in mid-1996, shortly after the arrival of the Ravens. The team played its first two years at Memorial Stadium. Although there was some sentiment from Baltimore residents in having the Ravens stay there permanently, it was deemed too old to host an NFL team. (The Orioles moved away from Memorial Stadium after the 1991 season.)

The stadium site was previously the site of the Wm. Knabe & Co. piano factory, which closed during The Great Depression. A sidewalk keyboard mosaic on the southwest corner of the stadium honors the company's legacy.

In 2003, M&T Bank acquired naming rights to the stadium. The bank had recently entered the Baltimore market with its purchase of Allfirst Bank. Two other companies were in the running to be granted naming rights to the stadium; they were reportedly Nextel and CarMax. Following the September 2002 death of Baltimore Colts quarterback Johnny Unitas, public sentiment leaned toward renaming the then-sponsorless stadium after the Baltimore icon. However, the Ravens and the Maryland Stadium Authority held firm in their right to negotiate naming rights fees. In the end, the plaza in front of the main entrance to the Ravens' stadium was named "Unitas Plaza", complete with a bronze statue of the Hall of Famer. The plaza formerly featured large banners, each containing a picture of Unitas in his playing days, flanking the stadium entrance. After 10 years, these were replaced by large metal 19s (Unitas's number) for the 2012 season. In 2014, the Ravens unveiled a new statue of long-time Raven Ray Lewis next to Unitas' statue. The bronze figure depicts Lewis in the final pose of his iconic "squirrel dance", which he would perform before every Ravens home game upon coming on to the field.

Mercedes-Benz Superdome

The Mercedes-Benz Superdome, often referred to simply as the Superdome, is a domed sports and exhibition venue located in the Central Business District of New Orleans, Louisiana. It primarily serves as the home venue for the New Orleans Saints of the National Football League, the home stadium for the Sugar Bowl, New Orleans Bowl in college football and the longtime rivalry football game of the SWAC Conference's Southern University and Grambling State University, known as the Bayou Classic (held yearly, every Thanksgiving Weekend). It also houses their schools' Battle of the Bands between The Southern University "The Human Jukebox" and Grambling State's Tiger Marching Band. Plans were drawn up in 1967 by the New Orleans modernist architectural firm of Curtis and Davis and the building opened as the Louisiana Superdome in 1975. Its steel frame covers a 13-acre (5.3 ha) expanse and the 273-foot (83 m) dome is made of a lamellar multi-ringed frame and has a diameter of 680 feet (210 m), making it the largest fixed domed structure in the world. It is adjacent to the Smoothie King Center.

Because of the building's size and location in one of the major tourist destinations of the United States, the Superdome routinely hosts major sporting events, including the Super Bowl, College Football Championship Games, and the Final Four in college basketball. The stadium was also the long-time home of the Tulane Green Wave football team of Tulane University until 2014 (when they returned on-campus at Yulman Stadium) and was the home venue of the New Orleans Jazz of the National Basketball Association (NBA) from 1975 until 1979.

The Superdome gained international attention of a different type in 2005 when it housed thousands of people seeking shelter from Hurricane Katrina. The building suffered extensive damage as a result of the storm, and was closed for many months afterward. It was eventually decided the building would be fully refurbished and reopened in time for the Saints' 2006 home opener on September 25.

On October 3, 2011, it was announced that German automaker Mercedes-Benz purchased naming rights to the stadium. The new name took effect on October 23, 2011.

Mercedes-Benz Stadium

Mercedes-Benz Stadium is a multi-purpose retractable-roof stadium located in Atlanta, Georgia. The home of the Atlanta Falcons and Atlanta United FC of Major League Soccer (MLS), it replaced the now-demolished Georgia Dome, the Falcons' home stadium from 1992 until 2016. Mercedes-Benz Stadium holds the record for the world's largest video board at 62,350 square feet (5,793 m2), and is one of five stadiums in the NFL with a retractable roof.

The stadium is owned by the state of Georgia through the Georgia World Congress Center Authority, and operated by AMB Group, the parent organization of the Falcons and Atlanta United. The total cost was estimated at US$1.6 billion, as of June 2016. The stadium officially opened on August 26, 2017 with a Falcons preseason game against the Arizona Cardinals, despite the retractable roof system being incomplete at the time. Work on the retractable roof was completed on July 14, 2018.

The Mercedes-Benz Stadium's projected opening date was delayed three times due to the complexity of the eight-panel retractable roof. The stadium was originally intended to open on March 1, 2017; however, the opening date was later delayed to June 1, 2017, then to July 30, 2017, and then to August 26, 2017. Steve Cannon, CEO of the Atlanta Falcons' parent company AMB Group, stated that the Falcons' preseason schedule and the Chick-fil-a Kickoff Games would not be affected by the new opening date; however, three of Atlanta United's matches would be affected. The July 30 game against Orlando City SC was moved to Atlanta United's interim home of Bobby Dodd Stadium for July 29 while two home matches scheduled in August were moved to later dates. Additionally, the Georgia Dome's demolition was put on hold until the new stadium's certificate of occupancy could be issued. On June 9, 2017, stadium officials announced that they were confident that Mercedes-Benz Stadium would open as scheduled, and demolition of the Georgia Dome had resumed, and the Dome was imploded on the morning of November 20, 2017.

On July 25, 2017, stadium officials reported that the roof would be in the closed position during the Falcons' preseason games and the Chick-fil-A Kickoff games while contractors continue to fine tune the roof to allow all eight panels to work in sync. Falcons' President Rich McKay also stated that the roof would remain closed whenever outside temperatures exceed 80 °F (27 °C). On August 16, 2017, WXIA reported that construction of the retractable roof system was intentionally delayed by stadium and construction officials to ensure the roof's long term operability and to ensure that other parts of the stadium would be completed on time.

On September 10, 2017, the Falcons announced that, contrary to earlier plans, the stadium roof would in fact be open during the Falcons home opener on September 17 against the Green Bay Packers if weather permitted. On October 6, 2017, stadium officials announced that the roof would be opened, weather permitting, for Atlanta United's regular season finale against Toronto FC on October 22; stadium officials also stated that the roof would remain closed for the remainder of the Falcons' regular season as well as for any home matches hosted by Atlanta United during the 2017 MLS Cup Playoffs as contractors continue to work on fully mechanizing the roof.

MetLife Stadium

MetLife Stadium is located in East Rutherford, New Jersey, 8 miles (13 km) outside of New York City. It is part of the Meadowlands Sports Complex and serves as the home stadium for two National Football League franchises: the New York Giants and the New York Jets. The stadium is owned by the MetLife Stadium Company, a joint venture of the Giants and Jets, who jointly built the stadium using private funds on land owned by the New Jersey Sports and Exposition Authority. The stadium opened as New Meadowlands Stadium in 2010. In 2011, MetLife, an insurance company based in New York City, acquired the naming rights to the stadium. At a construction cost of approximately $1.6 billion, it was the most expensive stadium ever built at the time that it opened.

MetLife Stadium is currently the only NFL stadium shared by two clubs. In 2020, it will be joined by Los Angeles Stadium at Hollywood Park in Inglewood, California which will be home to the Rams and Chargers. Los Angeles' Staples Center, which is home to the Clippers and the Lakers of the National Basketball Association (NBA), is the only other facility to currently house two teams from the same sports league in the United States. It has most recently featured WrestleMania 35.

As Giants Stadium approached 30 years of age, it was becoming one of the older stadiums in the NFL. The Jets, who had been the tenants at the stadium, sought to have their own stadium built in Manhattan proper, the proposed West Side Stadium. Originally intended to be the 85,000-seat main stadium for New York's bid for the 2012 Summer Olympics, it was designed to be downsized to 75,000 seats for the Jets. However, the West Side Stadium would have required significant public funding, which collapsed in 2005 mostly due to a vicious smear campaign orchestrated by Cablevision who feared the new venue would take business away from Madison Square Garden. The Jets then entered into a joint venture with the Giants to build a new stadium in which the two teams would be equal partners.

New Era Field

New Era Field, originally Rich Stadium, is in Orchard Park, New York, a suburb south of Buffalo. Opened in 1973, it is the home of the Buffalo Bills of the National Football League. New Era Cap Company holds the stadium's naming rights.

An original franchise of the American Football League in 1960, the Buffalo Bills played their first thirteen seasons at War Memorial Stadium, a multi-use WPA project stadium that opened in 1938, located on Buffalo's East Side. While suitable for AFL play in the 1960s, the "Rockpile" (as the stadium came to be nicknamed), was in disrepair and with a capacity of under 47,000, undersized for a National Football League team. The league mandate instituted after the AFL–NFL merger of 1970 dictated a minimum of 50,000 seats.

In early 1971, owner Ralph Wilson was exploring options to relocate the team, possibly to Seattle, with other cities such as Memphis and Tampa soon expressing interest as well. The potential loss of the team hastened the stadium project and Rich Stadium opened in 1973. The location and construction of the stadium in Erie County were the source of years of litigation, which ended with a financial settlement for a developer who had planned to erect a domed stadium in Lancaster. However, plans changed because it was not wanted to be close to Lancaster High School. The stadium was ultimately built by Frank Schoenle and his construction company. Bonds were approved by the county legislature in September 1971.

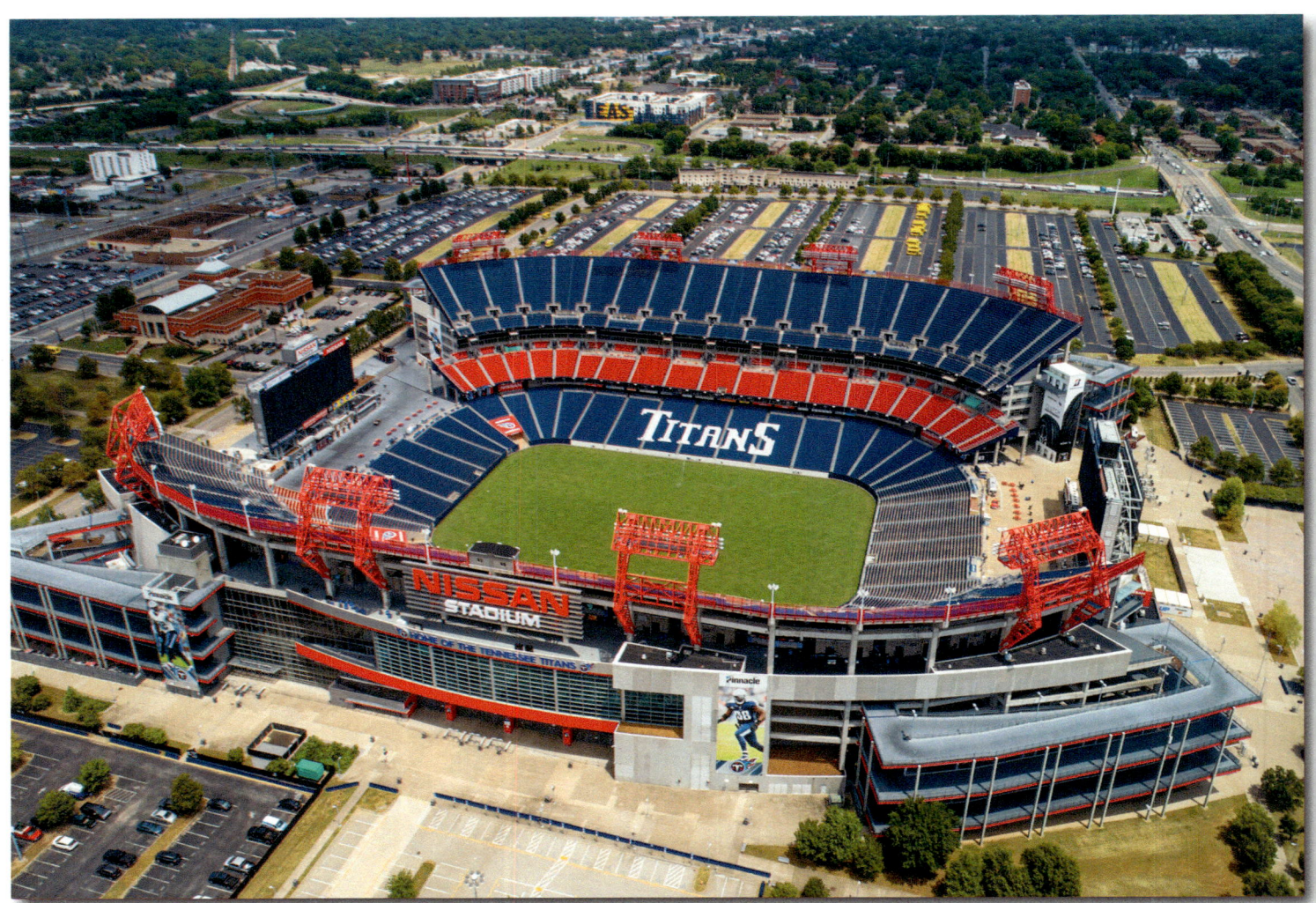

Nissan Stadium

Nissan Stadium is a multi-purpose stadium in Nashville, Tennessee. Owned by the Metropolitan Government of Nashville and Davidson County, it is primarily used for football and is the home field of the Tennessee Titans and the Tennessee State Tigers of Tennessee State University. The stadium is also the site of the Franklin American Mortgage Music City Bowl, a postseason college football bowl game played each December, and is occasionally used as a venue for soccer matches. Nissan Stadium is even used for large concerts, such as the CMA Music Festival nightly concerts, which take place for four days every June. Facilities are included to enable the stadium to host other public events, meetings, parties, and gatherings.

Nissan Stadium is located on the east bank of the Cumberland River, directly across the river from downtown Nashville and has a listed seating capacity of 69,143. Its first event was a preseason game between the Titans and the Atlanta Falcons on August 27, 1999. Since opening in 1999, it has been known by multiple names, including Adelphia Coliseum (1999–2002), The Coliseum (2002–2006), and LP Field (2006–2015).

The stadium features three levels of seating, with the lower bowl completely encompassing the field. The club and upper levels form the stadium's dual towers, rising above the lower bowl along each sideline. All of the stadium's luxury suites are located within the towers. Three levels of suites are located in the stadium's eastern tower: one between the lower and club levels, and two between the club and upper levels. The western tower has only two levels of suites, both between the club and upper levels. The pressbox is located between the lower and club levels in the western tower. Nissan Stadium's dual videoboards are located behind the lower bowl in each end zone.

The playing surface of Nissan Stadium is Tifsport Bermuda Sod, a natural grass. However, the relatively warm climate of Nashville, combined with the wear and tear of hosting a game nearly every weekend, usually results in a resodding of the area "between the hashes" in late November.

On Nissan Stadium's eastern side is the Titans Pro Shop, a retail store which sells team merchandise. It remains open year-round and maintains an exterior entrance for use on non-event dates.

NRG Stadium

NRG Stadium, formerly Reliant Stadium, is located in Houston, Texas. It was constructed at the cost of $352 million and has a seating capacity of 71,995. It was the first NFL facility to have a retractable roof.

The stadium is the home of the National Football League's Houston Texans, the Houston Livestock Show and Rodeo, the Texas Bowl, many of the United States men's national soccer team's matches, and other events. The stadium served as the host facility for Super Bowls XXXVIII (2004) and LI (2017), and WrestleMania XXV (2009).

NRG Stadium is part of a collection of venues (including the Astrodome), which are collectively called NRG Park. The entire complex is named for NRG Energy under a 32-year, US$300 million naming rights deal in 2000.

The Houston NFL Holdings group came to Populous (then HOK Sport) to begin the schematic design for the first-ever NFL retractable roof football stadium in 1997. The intention was to create a football stadium to replace the Astrodome that would operate like an open-air facility but have the intimacy and comfort of an indoor arena. With the design for football and the square footage requirements of the rodeo, the building was designed in the 1,900,000-square-foot (180,000 m2) range. Groundbreaking for the stadium was on March 9, 2000 and the building was officially topped off in October 2001. The stadium opened on August 24, 2002, with a preseason game between the Miami Dolphins and Houston Texans which the Dolphins won 24–3. The stadium hosted its first regular season NFL football game between the Dallas Cowboys and the Houston Texans on September 8, 2002. Construction was completed in 30 months. The first rodeo was held in the stadium in February 2003.

During a Texans preseason game on August 30, 2012, against the Minnesota Vikings, an intoxicated fan fell to his death from an escalator.

During the 2015 season, a permanent artificial surface was installed at NRG Stadium. The Texans had used a natural surface since the stadium opened, using a system of trays of sod similar to one used at Giants Stadium in its experiment with using a grass surface. In recent years, the stadium installed artificial turf to be used during high school and college games while keeping the grass for Texans games. After the Texans' home opener, complaints about the field conditions finally led to the installation of the artificial surface for Texans games. The surface brand is UBU Speed, which is part of Act Global.

In 2017, NRG Stadium selected Hellas Construction to install its Matrix Turf with Helix Technology at the stadium. The three year contract calls for a new turf field each year.

After hosting Super Bowl LI, further upgrades were made to keep NRG Stadium competitive with other new NFL venues. The stadium's first major renovation in 15 years modernized the office and team facilities.

Oakland–Alameda County Coliseum

The Oakland–Alameda County Coliseum, often referred to as the Oakland Coliseum, is a multi-purpose stadium in Oakland, California, which is home to the Oakland Athletics of Major League Baseball (MLB). The Coliseum was also home to some games of the San Jose Earthquakes of Major League Soccer in 2008–2009 and hosted games at the 2009 CONCACAF Gold Cup. The Oakland–Alameda County Coliseum complex consists of the stadium and the neighboring Oracle Arena.

The Coliseum has 6,300 club seats, 2,700 of which are available for Athletics games, 143 luxury suites, 125 of which are available for Athletics games, and a variable seating capacity of 46,867 for baseball, 56,057 for American football, and 63,132 for association football. In seating capacity, Oakland Coliseum is the second smallest NFL stadium, larger only than Dignity Health Sports Park, the temporary home of the Los Angeles Chargers, but the eighth largest MLB stadium.

On April 3, 2017, Opening Day, the Athletics dedicated the Coliseum's playing surface as Rickey Henderson Field in honor of MLB Hall of Famer and former Athletic Rickey Henderson.

The Coliseum features an underground design where the playing surface is actually below ground level (21 feet/6 meters below sea level). Consequently, fans entering the stadium find themselves walking on to the main concourse of the stadium at the top of the first level of seats. This, combined with the hill that was built around the stadium to create the upper concourse, means that only the third deck is visible from outside the park. This gives the Coliseum the illusion of being a short stadium from the outside.

Paul Brown Stadium

Paul Brown Stadium is located in Cincinnati, Ohio. It is the home venue of the Cincinnati Bengals and opened on August 19, 2000. Named after the Bengals' founder Paul Brown, the stadium is located on approximately 22 acres (8.9 ha) of land and has a listed seating capacity"of 65,515. Paul Brown Stadium is nicknamed "The Jungle," an allusion not only to the namesake Bengal tiger's natural habitat, but also the Guns N' Roses song "Welcome to the Jungle".

In 1996 Hamilton County voters passed a one-half percent sales tax increase to fund the building of two new home venues for both the Bengals and the Major League Baseball Cincinnati Reds. Previously the Bengals and the Reds shared tenancy of Riverfront Stadium (Cinergy Field), but both teams complained that the aging multipurpose facility lacked modern amenities and other things necessary for small-market teams to survive. Paul Brown Stadium was built first to the west; after the Bengals moved, Cinergy Field installed natural grass and was partially demolished to allow construction of adjacent Great American Ball Park to the east. Following the 2002 baseball season, Cinergy was demolished on December 29. The Bengals have hosted four NFL playoff games at Paul Brown Stadium, with no victories.

For its first four years the field was natural Kentucky Bluegrass, but maintenance problems arose, and at one point it was rated as the third-worst field in the league. Hamilton County explored other options and chose the synthetic FieldTurf system. The infilled artificial turf looks and feels like real grass and, since the field markings are sewn into the fabric, repainting between games is unnecessary. The reduced maintenance saved the county approximately US$100,000 annually. Additionally, it opens Paul Brown Stadium to other uses without worry of damage to the turf. The FieldTurf was installed for the 2004 season. The field is one of only two stadiums in the NFL to have "five miles of piping" running under the field to keep the rubber inlays heated. In April 2012, the stadium chose to update the playing surface with an installation of Act Global synthetic turf. In 2018, the stadium was equipped with a new top-of-the-line synthetic turf system. Manufactured by Shaw Sports Turf, the product includes Strenexe XD slit-film fibers that are supported by the strongest synthetic turf backing in the industry, UltraLoc.

Two LED video displays at either end zone, installed in 2000, provide a good view of the on-field action for every spectator. Over 200 feet of ribbon display were installed along the fascia of the stadium.

Raymond James Stadium

Raymond James Stadium was built to replace Tampa Stadium at the demand of the new Bucs owner Malcolm Glazer. It is located adjacent to the site of the old stadium on the former location of Al Lopez Field, a minor-league baseball stadium that had been demolished in 1989. Once completed, the final cost of the new stadium was $168.5 million, with the entire cost publicly financed.

It was known as Tampa Community Stadium during construction, but the naming rights were bought for US$32.5 million for a 13–year deal by St. Petersburg-based Raymond James Financial in June 1998. On April 27, 2006, an extension was signed to maintain naming rights through 2015. In May 2016 the Buccaneers announced that the naming rights were extended an additional 12 years ensuring that Raymond James Financial's name will continue to appear through 2028.

The stadium officially opened on September 20, 1998, when the Tampa Bay Buccaneers defeated the Chicago Bears, 27–15. The stadium hosted its first soccer game on March 20, 1999, when the Tampa Bay Mutiny lost to D.C. United, 5–2.

The stadium also hosts the annual Outback Bowl college football post-season game on New Year's Day since 1999. The Gasparilla Bowl will be held at the venue starting with the 2018 edition.

The stadium was selected to host the ACC Championship Game in 2008 and 2009.

The stadium is home field for the University of South Florida Bulls of the American Athletic Conference. The team's record crowd at Raymond James Stadium is 69,383, on September 29, 2012, when the Bulls – during their worst season ever – played a non-conference game against the popular Florida State University Seminoles from the powerhouse Atlantic Coast Conference for the first time.

The largest crowd ever recorded in Raymond James Stadium came on January 9, 2017 as the stadium hosted the 2017 College Football Playoff National Championship. 74,512 people were in attendance.

Through to the 2009 season, every Buccaneers game at Raymond James Stadium sold out. In 2010, no home game achieved a ticket sell out, so none could be broadcast on local television. The streak carried over until week four of the 2011 season, when it sold enough tickets for its Monday night game with the Indianapolis Colts on October 3 to avoid a local blackout.

Soldier Field

Soldier Field is located in the Near South Side of Chicago, Illinois. It opened in 1924 and is the home field of the Chicago Bears, who moved there in 1971. With a football capacity of 61,500, it is the third-smallest stadium in the NFL. In 2016, Soldier Field became the second-oldest stadium in the league when the Los Angeles Rams began playing temporarily at the Los Angeles Memorial Coliseum, which opened a year earlier than Soldier Field.

The stadium's interior was mostly demolished and rebuilt as part of a major renovation project in 2002, which modernized the facility but lowered seating capacity, while also causing it to be delisted as a National Historic Landmark. Soldier Field has served as the home venue for a number of other sports teams in its history, including the Chicago Cardinals of the NFL, University of Notre Dame football, and the Chicago Fire of Major League Soccer, as well as games from the 1994 FIFA World Cup, the 1999 FIFA Women's World Cup, and multiple CONCACAF Gold Cup championships. In 1968, it hosted the first Games of the Special Olympics.

The stadium hosted its first football game, on October 4, 1924, between Louisville Male High School and Chicago's Austin Community Academy High School. Louisville's team won 26–0. (Chicago Tribune, October 2, 1924)

Over 100,000 spectators attended the 1926 Army–Navy Game. It would decide the national championship, as Navy entered undefeated and Army had lost only to Notre Dame. The game lived up to its hype, and even though it ended in a 21–21 tie, Navy was awarded the national championship.

The all-time collegiate attendance record of 123,000+ was established November 26, 1927, as Notre Dame beat the University of Southern California 7–6. In 2016, 150,000+ attended a game between Virginia Tech and Tennessee at Bristol Speedway.

Austin defeated Leo to win the 1937 Prep Bowl; another contender for the highest attendance ever (estimated at over 120,000 spectators). The Chicago Prep Bowl games are held at Soldier Field yearly on the day after Thanksgiving. The bowl game is older than the IHSA state championship tournament held since the 1960s.

The stadium was host to 41 College All-Star Games, an exhibition between the previous year's NFL champion (or, in its final years, Super Bowl champion) and a team of collegiate all-star players prior to their reporting to their new professional teams training camps. This game was discontinued after the 1976 NFL season. The final game in 1976 was halted in the third quarter when a torrential thunderstorm broke out and play was never resumed.

In 2012, Notre Dame hosted a game at Soldier Field against the University of Miami as part of their Shamrock Series.

State Farm Stadium

State Farm Stadium, formerly known as University of Phoenix Stadium, is a multi-purpose football stadium located in Glendale, Arizona, west of Phoenix. It is the home of the Arizona Cardinals and the annual Fiesta Bowl. It replaced Tempe's Sun Devil Stadium as the Valley of the Sun's main stadium. The stadium is adjacent to the Gila River Arena, home of the Arizona Coyotes NHL team.

The stadium has hosted the Fiesta Bowl, the 2007, 2011 and 2016 College Football Playoff National Championships, Super Bowl XLII in 2008, the Pro Bowl and Super Bowl XLIX in 2015, and will host Super Bowl LVII in 2023. It was one of the stadiums for the 2015 CONCACAF Gold Cup and the Copa América Centenario in 2016. It hosted the NCAA Final Four in 2017 and will do so again in 2024.

The University of Phoenix acquired the naming rights in September 2006, shortly after the stadium had opened under the name Cardinals Stadium and retained the rights until September 2018 when State Farm acquired the naming rights. The Cardinals and State Farm reached agreement on an 18-year commitment that resulted in the team's home venue becoming State Farm Stadium.

Since moving to Arizona from St. Louis, Missouri in 1988, the Cardinals had played at Sun Devil Stadium on the campus of Arizona State University. The Cardinals had only planned to play there until a new stadium could be built in Phoenix. However, the savings and loan crisis derailed funding for a new stadium during the 1990s. Over time, the Cardinals expressed frustration at being merely tenants in a college football stadium. The lack of having their own stadium denied them additional revenue streams available to other NFL teams. The Cardinals campaigned several times in the years prior to its construction for a new and more modern facility.

The ceremonial groundbreaking for the new stadium was held on April 12, 2003, and the 63,400-seat stadium opened on August 1, 2006 after three years of construction. The stadium was designed by Eisenman Architects and HOK Sport (now Populous). The stadium is considered an architectural icon for the region and was named by Business Week as one of the 10 "most impressive" sports facilities on the globe due to the combination of its retractable roof (engineering design by Walter P Moore) and roll-in natural grass field, similar to the GelreDome and the Veltins-Arena.

LED video and ribbon displays from Daktronics in Brookings, South Dakota were installed in 2006 prior to Arizona's first game of the season at the new stadium. The cost of the project was $455 million. That total included $395.4 million for the stadium, $41.7 million for site improvements, and $17.8 million for the land. Contributors to the stadium included the Arizona Sports and Tourism Authority ($302.3 million), the Arizona Cardinals ($143.2 million), and the City of Glendale ($9.5 million).

TIAA Bank Field

TIAA Bank Field is located in Jacksonville, Florida, and primarily serves as the home facility of the Jacksonville Jaguars. The stadium opened in 1995 as Jacksonville Municipal Stadium on the site of the old Gator Bowl Stadium (erected 1927), and included some portions of the older stadium. Located on the St. Johns River, it sits on 10 acres (4.0 ha) of land in downtown Jacksonville.

In addition to hosting the Jaguars, the stadium is also regularly used for college football, concerts, and other events. It is the regular site of the annual Florida–Georgia game, a college football rivalry game between the University of Florida and the University of Georgia. The stadium is also the home of the annual Gator Bowl, a post-season college bowl game. Additionally, the stadium hosted Super Bowl XXXIX in 2005 and is one of the venues used by the United States men's national soccer team.

From 1997 to 2006, the stadium was named Alltel Stadium after communications company Alltel purchased naming rights. The facility was renamed EverBank Field in 2010, following the approval of a five-year, naming rights deal with the financial services company EverBank. The agreement was extended in 2014 for an additional 10 years. The Jaguars announced in February 2018 the stadium would be renamed TIAA Bank Field for the 2018 NFL season after EverBank was acquired by New York-based TIAA.

The stadium's re-opening day was also the home debut of the Jaguars during the 1995 NFL season. It was the first time that an expansion NFL team had played its first game in a new facility; they played the Houston Oilers in the opener and lost 10–3. The Gator Bowl returned as a New Year's Day bowl game on January 1, 1996, following the 1995 NCAA season.

In 1997, the stadium changed its name to Alltel Stadium after naming rights were acquired by Alltel, a telecommunications company best known as a wireless carrier. The name Alltel Stadium stopped being used by the city after January 2007 when the contract expired; by that point, most of Alltel's assets had been purchased by Verizon.

Super Bowl XXXIX

In 2005, the stadium hosted Super Bowl XXXIX in which the New England Patriots defeated the Philadelphia Eagles 24–21 in front of 78,125, the largest Super Bowl in attendance since 1994. Paul McCartney performed at halftime, performing Beatles classics "Drive My Car", "Get Back", and "Hey Jude", as well as a firework-filled "Live and Let Die". In 2003 and 2004, $47 million in improvements to the stadium were implemented to prepare for the Super Bowl. These improvements included the addition of a unique sports bar in the south end zone called the "Bud Zone", a larger and wider video and scoring display from Daktronics, escalators in the north and south end zone, and a new "terrace suite" called the "Sky Patio" right above the "Bud Zone" in the south end zone.

U.S. Bank Stadium

U.S. Bank Stadium is an enclosed stadium in Minneapolis, Minnesota. Built on the former site of the Hubert H. Humphrey Metrodome, the indoor stadium opened in 2016 and is the home of the Minnesota Vikings; it also hosts early season college baseball games of the University of Minnesota Golden Gophers (NCAA).

The Vikings played at the Metrodome from 1982 until its closure in 2013; during construction, the Vikings played two seasons (2014, 2015) at the open-air TCF Bank Stadium on the campus of the University of Minnesota. The team's first home was Metropolitan Stadium in Bloomington (1961–1981), now the site of the Mall of America.

On June 17, 2016, U.S. Bank Stadium was deemed substantially complete by contractor Mortenson Construction, six weeks before the ribbon-cutting ceremony and official grand opening on July 22. Authority to use and occupy the stadium was handed over to the Vikings and the Minnesota Sports Facilities Authority. The Vikings played their first pre-season game at U.S. Bank Stadium on August 28; the home opener of the regular season was in week two against the Green Bay Packers on September 18, a 17–14 victory.

It is the first fixed-roof stadium built in the NFL since Ford Field in Detroit, which opened in 2002. As of March 2015, the overall budget was estimated to be $1.061 billion, with $348 million from the state of Minnesota, $150 million from the city of Minneapolis, and $551 million from the team and private contributions.

U.S. Bank Stadium hosted Super Bowl LII won by the Philadelphia Eagles on February 4, 2018, the ESPN X Games on July 19–22, 2018, and the NCAA Final Four won by the Virginia Cavaliers on April 6–8, 2019. The stadium is also expected to host the 2020 NCAA Division I Wrestling Championships.

CURRENT TOP 10

Tom Brady

Career

Sportswriters and analyst have considered Tom Brady to be the greatest quarterback in NFL history. His six Super Bowl wins amongst various other football accomplishments during his nineteen-year career with the New England Patriots has proved him to be one of the "biggest steals" in the NFL's drafting history. In the 2000 NFL draft Brady was the overall 199th pick of the draft chosen in the 6th round by the New England Patriots. Brady not only holds various records for his outstanding play but his nineteen years playing for the Patriots sets another NFL record for the longest time a quarterback has ever played for one team. Since he became the Patriots starting quarterback in 2001 the Patriots have yet to have a losing season after having won sixteen divisional titles. This only sets yet another NFL record for the quarterback as no other player in the league's history to date has been able to accomplish the same. After winning the Superbowl for the Patriots in 2001 he became the second, after Kurt Warner, quarterback in NFL history to win the championship in his first season as a starter.

The first of the AFC championship games the Patriots played with Brady as their starting quarterback had him lead the team to victory going on to win the Superbowl XXXVI that same year. Including the 2001 AFC victory he has taken the Patriots to thirteen championship games of which they have won nine. Eight of those victory were consecutive ones spanning from 2011 to 2018. Of those eight AFC victories, the Patriots won six Superbowl's led by their star quarterback Tom Brady.

Until such time as another quarterback reaches two-hundred regular season wins he will stand in NFL history as the quarterback with the most NFL wins to-date. He has the most Superbowl wins of any player, he has the most NFL appearances than any other player and holds the record for first all-time playoff wins with a record postseason of 30-10. He holds the record with Wes Welker for the longest touchdown pass at ninety-nine yards.

At the age of forty-one, Tom Brady is also the oldest quarterback in the NFL's history to have won a Superbowl. In 2016 his shiny record was besmirched by the alleged accusations of his involvement in the Deflategate football tampering scandal for which he suffered a suspension. He missed the first four games of the 2016 season after which he went on to once again take the Patriots to a Superbowl victory.

Personal Information

Born Thomas Edward Patrick Brady Jr. on August 3, 1977, to Thomas Brady, Snr. And Galynn Patricia, nee Johnson. He was the only son and fourth child having three older sisters Nancy, Julie and Maureen the grew up in a Catholic home. The forty-one-year-old quarterback for the Patriots has played for no other NFL team since his draft in 2000.

Early Years

From the age of four Brady has been a fan of Joe Montana who became his inspiration and idol having first seen Montana in the 1981 NFC Championship game. He bore witness to the 49ers beat the Dallas Cowboys and Joe Montana throw what was dubbed "The Catch" to Dwight Clark.

Brady was taught to throw a football at the College of San Mateo football camp by the camp counselor Tony Graziani. Graziani went on to be an NFL League player for the Atlanta Falcons. As he grew up Brady became a fan of the Boston Celtics and Los Angeles Lakers.

He attended Junipero Serra High School in San Mateo where he played basketball, football and baseball graduating in 1995. His football career began playing for the Padres junior varsity team where he was not given the starting position until the quarterback was injured. Before he took over as a starter the team had yet to win a game. He remained the team's starter until he graduated.

But football was not the only sport at which Brady excelled, and the Montreal Expos picked him in the 18th round of the 1995 MLB draft. The offered him an excellent package akin to what they would have offered an early 3rd round pick as he had so impressed the MLB scouts. But he was determined that football was the way he wanted to go and signed up with the University of Michigan after being recruited by Bill Harris. His high school football career was finished off with him having 31 touchdowns and completing 236 of 447 passes for 3702 yards. His varsity career led him to hone his football skills, even more, leading to where he currently stands today as one of the NFL's greatest quarterbacks of all time.

CURRENT TOP 10

Antonio Brown

Career

Pittsburgh Steelers wide receiver Antonio Tavaris Brown holds the record for most receiving yards and receptions than any other player ever has in the NFL. He was a sixth-round pick drafted in 2010 as the 195th pick that year.

He has been with the Pittsburgh Steelers since 2010 where the team went all the way to the Super Bowl XLV in his first season but were beaten by the Green Bay Packers.

Antonia was both a track star and football player through high school where he attended Miami Norland High School having been raised in Liberty City, Miami. After high school, he went to Michigan University. In 2008 and 2009 he won the All-American honors as a punt runner. Having finished his first (rookie) season on a high with 16 receptions for 167 yards. This was within ten games he then went on to end his second season with over 1000 yards for both returning and receiving becoming the only NFL player to have ever achieved this. In the 2012 Pro Bowl, he was chosen a punt returner. He had a $42.5 million 5-year extension (including an $8.5 million sign up bonus) to sign with the Steelers. Brown was noted as the only receiver to ever record 5 receptions within 50 yards in the history of the NLF He was rewarded for his outstanding playing performance in 2017 when the Steelers signed him for another 5-year contract which will take him through to 2021.

Personal Information

Antonio Brown was born on the 10th July 1988 and is the son of Eddie Brown, who played at the wide receiver for Louisiana Tech, collegiate football. Antonio's father also played the same position for Firebirds in the Arena Football League where he was voted as the best player in the league's history.

Early Years

Antonio was both a track and football star at Miami Norland High School in Florida. During his years in high school, he played a few football positions including quarterback, running back, punt returner and wide receiver.

After being turned down due to academic concerns by Florida State University he started attending North Carolina Tech Prep. Florida International University offered him a scholarship he was not here for long when he was expelled. He joined Central Michigan where Butch Jones, a coach that tried to recruit him whilst he worked for West Virginia, had begun working. He started his football career here as a walk-on freshman. He played for Central Michigan from 2007 to 2009. He did not play his senior season at Central Michigan as he started playing for the NFL.

CURRENT TOP 10

Carson Wentz

Career

Carson Wentz is the current quarterback for the Philadelphia Eagles. He was the overall second pick of the first round in the 2016 NFL Draft. His football career with the NFL has seen him have three NFL records, including that of Most Pass completions by a rooking (he had 379), Most pass completions in the 24 games he has played in his career (this stands at 540). He has so far surpassed the record held by Matty Ryan for the most consecutive games with a 1+ TD pass with 1 INT or less.

He holds six Eagles franchise records as well as six Awards which include the Super Bowl champion (LII), Pro Bowl in 2017, Bert Bell Award in 2017, two NFC Offensive Player of the week awards for weeks 1 and 7 in 2016. Three Pepsi Rook of the Week awards for weeks for weeks 1,3 and 7 in 2016, NFC Offensive Rookie of the Month in September of 2016 and NFC Offensive Player of the Month in October 2017.

Wentz led the Eagles to a very strong 2017 season start with a record of 11 – 2 but could not finish the season missing the last three games due to a knee injury. Wentz won a championship ring that year as the Eagles went of the have their first Super Bowl win (Super Bowl LII) beating the Patriots 41 – 33.

Personal Information
Carson Wentz was born on the 30th December 1992 in Raleigh North Carolina. His, family moved to North Dakota when he was three years old. He attended Century High School which is in Bismarck where he played both basketball and baseball (he played for the Patriots). As a senior Wentz has a growth spurt taking him from 5' 8" as a freshman to 6'5". He graduated from high school as valedictorian of his class in 2011.

Early Years

In his first year of college, where he attended North Dakota, he was redshirted with the Bison. The Bison got to win their first FCS title that year (2011) coached by head coach Craig Bohl. In 2012 as a college freshman, Wentz was the backup quarterback getting to play his first collegiate game as Brock Jensen's relief on the 22 September 2012 The Bison had a blowout victory over the Prairie View A&M Panthers of 66 – 7. Wentz went on to have two touchdowns and completed 12 of 16 pass attempts for 144 yards that season.

His 2013 season had him once again playing as the backup quarterback to Brock Jensen and had one of his best seasons. He played 11 games and ended this season (which was his sophomore season) completing 22 of 30 passes for 209 yards with one touchdown.

He became the starting quarterback for the Bison's in 2014 and started all 16 games that season. He got his first career high in his senior year at NDU in 2015 as he passed 335 yards in a game against Northern Iowa.

Julio Jones

Career

Julio Jones is an all-around incredible athlete with his 6'3" frame weighing 220 lbs. he exhibits speed, agility, strength, and control. It is no surprise that he became the fastest NFL Player in history where in 104 games he managed to reach 10000 career receiving years. This is an average of 96.7 receiving yards for each game he has played and is the highest in the history of the NFL.

In 2015 Jones became a first-team All-Pro selection and has been invited to six Pro Bowls. In 2016 he was one of the main contenders to help lead the Falcons to the Super Bowl LI.

He led the league in receiving yards in 2017 and 2018 where he was named second-team All-Pro each of those years.

In 2011 Jones posted the longest long jump at the NFL Combine and took the third fastest title for the 40-yard dash amongst wide receivers whilst having with a broken bone in his foot.

In his first year with the Falcons, they made the 2011 Super bowl although they lost against the New York Giants that year. He still came out of the playoffs with 7 receptions for 64 yards.

Personal Information

Julio Jones was born on the 8th February 1989 in Foley Alabama. He attended Foley High School and went to Alabama college where he played for the Crimson Tide leading them to an undefeated season in his sophomore year (2009). He was also a star athlete in high school standing out as being exceptional at track. He became the state champ in the triple jump and long jump during high school in 2006 and again in 2007. In the same years, he became the Gatorade T&F Athlete of the Year. Amongst some of the awards, he won during 2006 and 2007 was Mr. Alabama Track & Field athlete of the year in 2007. In 2008 he got listed as the number 1 wide receiver in the nation.

Early Years

Jones was drafted to the NFL in 2011 deciding to leave college football in his senior opting to rather play for the NFL. He was drafted in round one as overall pick number 6 in 2011.

In his junior season, he had an Alabama record of 1,133 yards with 7 touchdowns and 78 catches. He held a few school records when he ended with Alabama and was a first-team ALL-SEC selection in 2010.

Rivals.com had Jones rated as a five-star recruit and the nation's number one wide receiver in 2008. He played for the Alabama Crimson Tides from 2008 until he was drafted by the Atlanta Falcons in 2011.

CURRENT TOP 10

Le 'Von Bell

Career

Le'Veon Bell was drafted by the Pittsburgh Steelers in the second round of the 2013 NFL Draft and was selected 48th overall that year. Giovani Bernard was the first running back to be selected that year as the overall 37th pick making Bell the second running back to be selected in 2013.

Bell was signed to a 4-year rookie contract for $4.12 million which included a signing bonus of $1.37 million. In his second pre-season game of 2013, he was tackled and suffered a foot injury. Although it did not require surgery, he had to miss the first three weeks of regular season games.

The Steelers lost to the Minnesota Vikings in his first career game of the season which was played in Wembley Stadium, London, October 2013. His first touchdown in the game was a first-quarter eight-yard run. This game saw him have two rushing touchdowns, catch 4 receptions for 27 yards and rushed 57 yards on 16 carries.

Bell broke Franco Harris's rookie record on December 29, 2013, for total yard from scrimmage. This he did with a total of 1259 yards against the Cleveland Browns.

His rookie season ended with him having started the last 13 games of the season. He had 8 rushing touchdowns, 244 carries, 860 rushing yards and 45 receptions for 399 yards.

After a good 2014 season of which he became an All-Pro and finished second in rushing yards, all-purpose yards and yards from scrimmage. He was beaten by DeMarco Murray from the Cowboys. His fellow players ranked him at number 16 for the NFL Top 100 Players of 2015 and he was named to the Pro Bowl.

Bell had a career low when he and one of his teammates, LeGarrette Blount were arrested on charges of possession of marijuana and a DUI. The NFL penalized him by suspending him from the regular seasons first four games of 2015. But the sentence was reduced to the first three and after an appeal, it was dropped to missing the first two games.

Bells 2015 season came to an end on the 1 November when he suffered a torn MCL. This happened in the game against the Cincinnati Bears during the second quarter. Linebacker Vontaze Burfict, the linebacker for the Bears, tackled him. He had to be put on injured reserved for the rest of the 2015 season. It was reported that he had to have surgery on his knee in November but by the 2016 offseason, Bell was ready to return to play.

In 2016 he was ranked 41st on the NFL Top 100 Players of 2016 list despite his injury.

He has won 3 Pro Bowl in years 2014, 2016 and 2017, 2 First Team All-Pro in 2014 and 2017, had a Second-Team All-Pro in 2016, Big Ten Championship in 2010 and First-Team All-American in 2012 as well as First-Team All-Big Ten in 2012.

Bell missed the first nine regular season games in 2018 as he refused to sign the Steelers Franchise tag. When contract negotiations started in July, he did not show up for any of the team activities and never reported to the Steelers by the league's deadline on November 13th. This made Bell ineligible to play in the 2018 NFL League Season. The Steelers have recently (20 February 2019) that Bell was not going to be franchise tagged. As such he will be a free agent for the new official NFL year upon the opening of the free agency on the 13th March 2019.

CURRENT TOP 10

Todd Gurley

Career

Started as a round one pick in the NFL draft of 2015 being picked 10th overall that year. In 2017 he was named the NFL Offensive Player of the year after he gained 19 offensive touchdowns in the 2017 season. He has played for the St. Louis / Los Angeles Rams since he was drafted in 2015 and is currently active on their roster.

Gurley got a suspension in 2014 by the University of Georgia for an alleged violation of NCAA rules. The two-day investigation in the allegations determined that the player had taken money in the amount of $3000 dollars over two years for various memorabilia sales. His suspension made Gurley miss a total of four games that season. In November 2014 at his first game played since his suspension, he tore his ACL effectively ending his junior football season.

In 2015 he entered the NFL Draft deciding not to finish his senior year. He became the and was the first running back to be selected that year. He could not play with the team during pre-season but still managed to practice and was medically cleared before in time for his 2015 rookie season.

In week 19 of the season, Gurley rushed for 85 yards in a victory over the Seattle Seahawks to become the second Rams rookie to have 10 touchdowns and rush for 1000 yards.

In his career, he has gone on to win 3 Pro Bowls in 2015, 2017 and 2018, NFL Offensive Player of the year in 2017. He holds 2 First-Team All-Pro selection for 2017 and 2018, 3 NFC Offensive Player of the Month titles, 5 NFC Offensive player of the week titles, FedEx Ground Player of the year for 2017, FedEx Ground Player of the week. He has been ranked No. 22 in the Top 100 Players for 2016 and no. 6 in 2018. He got the NFL Offensive Rookie of the Year title in 2015 and the PFWA All-Rookie Team in 2015.

Person Information

Born in Baltimore, Maryland on the 3rd August 1994 Todd Gerome Gurley II went to Tarboro High School in Tarboro, North Carolina. He was a top athlete at his school playing basketball, football, and track.

Early Years

In 2010 he was named the Rocky Mount Telegram All-Area Offensive Player of the year. He played for the Vikings as the running back and defensive back in his junior year. In his senior year, he was named the Player of the year in 2011 by the North Carolina Associated Press. He won this title for his 38 touchdowns and totaling 2600 yards.

He was also a top track and field star where he competed with Team USA. In the 2011 World Youth Championships in Athletics -he came third in 110-meters with the best time of 13.66 seconds. He finished overall 15th in the semi-finals and also partook in the 100-meter dash where he ran one of his best times of 10.70 second, placing 2nd in the prelims of the 2011 NCHSAA 2A State Track Meet.

He enrolled with the University of Georgia where he played football with head coach Mark Richt. Rivals.com listed him as a four-star recruit.

CURRENT TOP 10

Aaron Donald

Career

Ranked as one of the top defensive players in the NFL for his physical strength and having one the AP Defensive Player of the Year for two straight years in a row.

He was drafted in the 2014 NFL Draft in round one as overall pick number 13. He has spent his entire professional career playing for the St. Louis/Los Angeles Rams and is still active on their roster.

Donald has won many awards in his football career including the Lombardi Award, Bronko Nagurski Trophy, Chuck Bednarik Award and the Outland Trophy which he won in 2013 for a stellar season.

He set the record for the fastest 40-yard dash time with a 4.68 for a defensive tackle in the NFL Combine.

He was signed to a four-year $10.13 million contract which included a $5.69 million signing bonus with the Rams. His first career start was in October of 2014 in the game against the San Francisco 49ers. He came out of this game with four solo tackles. He was selected for the 2015 Pro Bowl and won the NFL Defensive Rookie of the Year award as well as being named to the NFL All-Rookie team.

Donald was ranked as no. 14 on the NFL Top 100 Players of 2016. The 2016 season saw Donald ejected for illegal contact with a referee and was fined $21269 for unnecessary roughness and unsportsmanlike conduct.

In 2017 he had numerous contract disputes and was fined $1.4 million for non-participation. He missed games and was fined $1.8 million for each game that he missed. In 2018 he signed a $135 million six years with a guaranteed $87 million contract extension. This has made him the highest earning defensive player in the history of the NFL.

Person Information

Aaron Charles Donald was born in Pittsburgh, Pennsylvania on the 23rd May 1991. He attended Penns Hills High School in Pittsburgh.

His father strength trained with him from the age of 12 to help build structure and move him from being an admittedly lazy kid. In high school, he played for football coach Ron Graham and was selected for the first team All-State Class AAAA for his two final seasons.

Rivals.com considered Aaron to be a three-star prospect and 37th best overall defensive tackle in the nation. He chose to go to Pittsburgh rather than accept other offers from the likes of Rutgers, Toledo, and Akron.

Early Years

His freshman year saw him play as a reserve defensive end where he recorded 11 tackles, three for loss and two sacks. As a sophomore in 2011, he played in the starting lineup where he was named a second-team All-Big East selection.

His senior year he became named as the ACC Defensive Player of the year and a unanimous All-American.

Drew Brees

Career

Brees started for the Chargers in 2002 making the Pro Bowl in 2004. He tore his rotator cuff and labrum as well as dislocated his shoulder in 2005. After his recovery from his injuries, he signed with the New Orleans Saints in 2006. He led the Saints to win the Super Bowl XLIV, which was their first ever Super Bowl win.

His career with the Saints has been a huge success for him as he holds many NFL quarterback records including those for passing yards, 300-yard games, and touchdowns. He also holds NFL career records for career passing yards, career pass completions, and career completion percentage.

He became the NFL's Come Back Player of the Year in 2004, Offensive Player of the Year in 2008 and again in 2011. He was the Super Bowl XLIV MVP and was named the 2010 Sports Man of the Year by Sports Illustrated.

Personal Information

Drew Brees was born on the 15th January 1979 in Austin, Texas. He attended West Lake High School in Austin. His father was a prominent Texas trial lawyer and his mother was an attorney. He has a younger brother and he married his college sweetheart in 2003 with whom he has four children.

Early Years

It was not until high school that Brees started to play tackle football where he was a varsity letterman in basketball, football, and baseball. In the 11th grade, he sustained a knee injury that had the college recruiters overlook him. He overcame an ACL tear in 1996 and was selected 5A Most Valuable Offensive Player for Texas High School. He went on to lead his high school to a 16-0 record reason and state championship.

Only Kentucky and Purdue colleges made Brees offers. He chose to Purdue for the excellent academic program from which he graduated with a degree in industrial management in 2001.

He played for the Purdue Boilermakers where he was given his first start during his sophomore year. During his junior and senior years, he was the offensive captain for the team. Although he was given the opportunity to be available for the NFL Draft in 2000 Brees wanted to complete his senior year.

Brees was drafted in the 2nd round, 32nd overall pick in the NFL Draft of 2001 by the San Diego Chargers. In 2006 as a free agent he joined the New Orleans Saints where he is currently active on their roster as the quarterback.

CURRENT TOP 10

Von Miller

Aaron Rodgers

Career

Von Miller was drafted in the 2011 NFL Draft by the Broncos in round one and 2nd overall. As a rookie he received the first-team All-Pro honors, has been selected seven times for Pro Bowl and is considered to be one of the best defenders in the NFL League.

He received the Super Bowl MVP award after the Broncos won the Super Bowl 50 over the Carolina Panthers. He has even appeared in the TV Series Dancing with the Stars (22nd season of the show).

He has an impressive first season and ranked 2nd at the 2011 NFL Combine in the 40-yard dash, 1st in the 60-yard shuttle where his 11.15-second shuttle broke a combine linebacker record.

In March of 2011, he was persuaded by LaDainian Tomlinson to represent rookies in the NFL Labor Union talks.

Miller signed with the Broncos on the 28 July 2011 after John Elway was reported saying "Miller is the type of guy who only comes around every ten years". After the draft selection of Miller came as a surprise to certain experts on the NFL Draft.

Miller was fined three times during his first season for various offenses but in his second season got off to an excellent start putting him inline as an MVP candidate.

He has won many an award during his career and including Super Bowl 50 Champion, Super Bowl 50 MVP, 7 Pro Bowl, 3 First-Team All-Pro to name but a few of his outstanding achievements.

In his 2018 season, he recorded his 100th career sack to become the NFL's 5th-fastest player. He has been selected the starting player outside linebacker which will be his fifth consecutive Pro Bowl and his seventh career one.

Career

Aaron Rodgers spent his first three seasons as a backup to Brett Favre making starting quarterback in the 2008 season. He earned the Super Bowl MVP award in the 2010 Super Bowl XLV for the victory over the Pittsburgh Steelers. In 2011 the Associated Press voted him as the Associated Press Athlete of the year and the league MVP (he was also voted league MVP again in 2014 NFL season).

He is only one of two league quarterbacks to have a regular season career passer rating that is over 100 and he is the fifth all-time postseason. He has some of the NFL's best passer ratings, lowest career interception percentages make some analyst suggest him to be one of the greatest quarterbacks of all time.

Person Information

Born in Chico California on the 2nd December 1983 and attended Pleasant Valley High School. He has two younger brothers, he was in a relationship with Olivia Munn from 2014 to 2017 and recently started dating Danica Patrick.

Early Years

Rogers was known for setting various records throughout his high-school football career but despite this, he did not get many offers at all for college. He has attributed this to his 5'10 stature and not very big build throughout high school. He applied to and was turned down for Florida State which was his number one choice to play for coach Bobby Bowden. After declining an invitation to a walk-on from Illinois he went on to play for Butte Community College in Oroville. Before which he was about to quit football to pursue a career in law.

He was found by Jeff Telford who had come to Butte to recruit Jeff Tedford for the California Golden Bears. In 2003 Rogers became a junior college transfer to the University of California. In the fifth game of the season, he became the starting quarterback and helped to lead the Bears to a 7 – 3 victory in his sophomore season.

In 2004 he led California to record 10 – 1 victory with only 1 loss in a game that he set a record for the most consecutive passes (23) in one game.

Aaron decided to join the NFL instead of playing his senior season at California. He entered the 2005 NFL Draft where he was overall pick 24 in the first round. He has been with the Green Bay Packers since his draft in 2005.